This Book is the Property of

If found, please don't return to

____

I'll do the lost and found casting (page 165)

Charm Casting

Divining with Trinkets, Trifles, Baubles, and Bits

TINA HARDT

This edition first published in 2025 by Weiser Books, an imprint of

Red Wheel/Weiser, LLC
With offices at:
65 Parker Street, Suite 7
Newburyport, MA 01950
www.redwheelweiser.com

ISBN: 978-1-57863-872-7

Library of Congress Cataloging-in-Publication Data

Names: Hardt, Tina, 1962- author.
Title: Charm casting : divining with trinkets, trifles, baubles, and bits / Tina Hardt.
Description: Newburyport, MA : Weiser Books, 2025. | Summary: "Written with warmth and humor, this is an accessible guidebook that takes you on an enchanted journey on the hows and whys of assembling casting kits. Long before the kitchen junk drawer or the trinket gumball machine was invented, shamans, healers, and seers would cast and read bones, shells, stones, coins, and nuts. Where and how these pieces landed could reveal great insight into the human condition and our eternal selves. Learn how to assemble, find meaning, and explore your future by casting an oracle made from bits and baubles attuned to your personal energies"-- Provided by publisher.
Identifiers: LCCN 2025008091 | ISBN 9781578638727 (trade paperback) | ISBN 9781633413641 (ebook)
Subjects: LCSH: Divination. | Oracles.
Classification: LCC BF1773 .H373 2025 | DDC 133.3/2--dc23/eng/20250815
LC record available at https://lccn.loc.gov/2025008091

Cover design by Sky Peck Design
Cover photograph © Eryn Eaton
Interior by Brittany Craig
Typeset in Change

Printed in the United States of America
IBI
10 9 8 7 6 5 4 3 2 1

Merry meet. Merry part. Merry meet again.

For Wesley Prince, who I'm told was a dog.
You're loved more and more every day, little man.

From there to here,
and here to there,
funny things are
everywhere.
—Dr. Seuss

Contents

ACKNOWLEDGMENTS

It must begin with you, Carrie Paris. Though the embodiment of humility in greatness, a few words still need to be said. I'm grateful in this lifetime to have been cast into your orbit for so many reasons. This book could not have been written without you. And, no doubt, you'll recognize your inimitable imprint. You've seeded devotion and discipline, but most heartening, the power of awe—because it's the skeleton key that ultimately unlocks new vistas. Next, to those sitters, friends, and kindred who inspire and support me by sharing their astounding insights, kind validation, or an implied *what the merry hell are you on about?* You send me back to the drawing board time and time again. Beloved Red Wheel/Weiser Books editors and designers, Amy Lyons, Kathryn Sky-Peck, Jane Hagaman, Christine LeBlond, and Brittany Craig, XXOO. Thank you for helping me *rite gooder*, and for honoring the Wee Ones with such lovely pages. Dearly and deeply, to my Captain Roger Carlsen, who unwittingly signed on for a life and house filled with words, spirits, hocus-pocus, and tiny, shiny things that bewitch, bother, and bewilder—I love you.

Pack a snack, dear Diviner, *and get ready to tumble down a rabbit hole and into the whimsical wonderland of charm casting. We, the author—that's me—and a cool cast of curios who eagerly await your attentions, are thrilled to meet you. There's a fun-drenched adventure ahead of you. This is where you'll learn how to create a uniquely personal and dynamic oracle, ask wise questions, then throw some of them—as many as you like—into the air. Oh yes, and here comes the best part: then you'll get to make sense of how they've all landed.*

You may notice that one trinket fell smack-dab in the center of your casting surface (which you've created, by the way), while another trifle is upside down and doesn't seem to want to talk (much). And what about that saucy bauble, the one that's rolled right off the table? Still, thank heavens for the bits that will be here, there, and everywhere ready to share their helpful and prophetic insights. Not only will charm casting make the hours seem like minutes, but it will also get you ready to increase your intuition and psychic abilities—not to mention your star quality. So what are you waiting for? Flip the page, and let's get your cast on.

—Tina Hardt

INTRODUCTION

SHARPEN YOUR PENCILS

Tell me and I forget. Teach me and I remember.
Involve me and I learn.
—Benjamin Franklin

Whether you're a newcomer getting curiouser and curiouser or a more seasoned stoic looking to expand, refine, or deepen your connection with your collection, welcome. Experience and skill levels aside, it's time to sharpen your pencils and dig out a nerdy cardigan because we're heading to charm school.

I can only imagine what my maternal grandfather must be thinking. He was an academic who spoke multiple languages, had a PhD in philosophy, and purportedly strolled the drafty corridors of the University of Vienna with the likes of Sigmund Freud. Yet instead of learning chess, reading Tolstoy, or studying Ukrainian like my cousins, I've dedicated a great deal of my limited intellect to contemplating how a miniature rubber ducky combines with a monkey to inform my future. OK, the lights just flickered—time to move on!

I was first introduced to divining with strange little things by Carrie Paris. Carrie released her *Magpie Oracle* in 2014. It was a round tin of tiny, shiny metallic charms that were cool to the touch and murmured when you swirled your fingers through them. They made me recall a stupid game I played as a kid with another bored boy. Our babysitter had a collection of small, ridged plastic coins in a bucket. We'd rummage through the coins weirdly enchanted by the sound, a siren's song that ultimately led to us repeatedly throwing them into the air just to hear them alight on the basement floor with a different medley every toss.

Eventually, Carrie and Andrew McGregor released a mediumship-themed charm casting kit. And this is where I really fell into the soup. The charms arrived in a cigar box tied with a piece of red and white butcher's twine. Unable to contain myself, I ran to find a pair of scissors, cut the cord, and threw it out. During the first online tutorial for the kit, they said to keep the twine because you'll be using it in your readings. *Facepalm.* The next day I headed out to our shed to see if I could replace this magical string. I opened the shed door and lowered my gaze, presumably to ensure I didn't trip over the wooden threshold. When I lifted my foot, I kid you not, there in the dirt was a length of black and white butcher's twine. After a few minutes spent frozen-in-the-headlights, I bolted back to add it to the box.

But it gets better . . .

Later *that* night, Roger called from the car. He was on his way home and had terrible news. There had been a fatal and tragic accident close to our home: that was all he said. I asked him not to give me any details. I sat meditatively, asked for permission, then connected. I did a casting. The twine—you know that's going to get my attention—landed in a spiral with other pieces, too many to explain here; but, incredibly, at the top, there it was. The key validating charm—a cycle. I was able to divine many details from this casting. I could tell from the way that the twine had landed where the accident had happened: just south of a roundabout less than ten minutes from where we live. I knew where the cyclist had come from and in what direction he was pedaling before he was hit. I felt that the hit-and-run was suspicious and that a female was involved. I also suspected that the police wouldn't have enough for a conviction.

This would lead to an intense and far-more-detailed divination that spanned months and led to some astounding third-party validations. A combination of cards, casting charms, and the most mind-blowing synchronicities culminated in one last incredible incident. I was shopping when a small event happened in the store. A cruiser arrived, and two young police officers showed up. They served and protected. All good. I just happened to be wearing an NYPD sweatshirt that I had bought while attending the Readers Studio. It caught their eye and we began chatting. Well, what were the chances? They worked with the detective that had been assigned to this investigation. Sadly, they confirmed it was still a cold case.

Despite everything I'd uncovered or learned, I'd been deeply troubled by my inability to help, to make a difference. At least, this twenty-year-old who had passed so tragically had crossed over and was at peace. That's the main thing. Still, what had been the overarching point of this entire divination? Why would this Spirit-guided trail of breadcrumbs turn soggy like weathered tributes left at a roadside memorial? If nothing else, this had been a deeply personal journey that had yielded two big lessons. First, sometimes it's just not meant to be. The universe has its own rhyme and reason. And second and most importantly, those tiny things rustling around in their tin . . . they have big voices. You just need to learn how to listen.

I have immeasurable respect for those who've taken on the mantle of mentor. I also maintain that you don't honor a great teacher by becoming a carbon copy. They've worked hard to share the legacy of their knowledge, and one day, you owe it to them to flap your wings and fly the hell out of their nest. It's my heartfelt wish that you connect with your own style, method, and madness. Lovingly agree? Passionately disagree? Either way, you're engaged, and that's the aim of this book. I hope you're sent on a few *how-am-I-going-to-explain-this-one* kinds of experiences, because this also venerates my teachers. If ever in doubt, petition that power of awe. Sometimes you just have to throw stuff in the air and see, feel, and hear how it lands for *you*.

I see you've made it this far. (*Thank you.*) So it is time to take a brief tour of the campus and curriculum. This project is, in part, a COVID baby. It was born from the climate and residual memory of isolation and the strain that having too much alone time placed on our well-being. So the content will not only be instructional but also inspirational and therapeutic. It will encourage you to play and to boldly find sanctuary in your own imagination, creativity, spirituality, and self-discovery. Remarkably, this can all be achieved with a dented tin filled to the brim with small and oddly compelling objects I call the Wee Ones.

This sprightly little book includes exercises, checklists, creative activities, tips, scribbles and musings, grimoire prompts, and sample readings all aimed at enjoying charm casting as a sense of occasion. Oh, you'll be busy. Yet time will fly because it's all about fun and fine divining, which, you'll soon discover, don't have to be mutually exclusive.

With all the inventive DIY work ahead, you'll really benefit from starting a journal. *I know:* In many cases, this is like telling a witch she'll need a broom. Your eyes have probably already darted to a shelf groaning under the weight of your recorded wisdom. That said, page 151 will present the case for keeping a binder-style grimoire dedicated exclusively to the Wee Ones, their expanding meanings and inventory, your escapades and reflections—even the odd picture. Why not? They grow up so fast . . .

Whether it takes a few hours or spans a lifetime, you'll learn how to build that one-and-only master kit or get new ideas for additional sets for hot themes such as relationships, self-care, yes/no, alignment, or manifestation. You'll also discover all of the best must-have and must-make accessories. Finding your charms will bring back the joy of a treasure hunt. Checklist in hand, you'll be sent out on a foray into nature, closets, junk drawers, antique and thrift stores, sewing boxes and handbags (hopefully your own). We'll also explore a more personalized approach and grand staging for your readings that will glow-up your charms beyond your wildest belief.

Just a quiet aside for our beginners: If you're a newbie, allow me to let you in on a little secret. If you don't have the time (or criminal instincts) to ransack your home and community for tiny treasures, it's very easy to buy some starter charms online. You just have to search for assorted metal charms that are used for making jewelry. And then, once bitten, you'll gradually consider swapping out, adding, or removing pieces. And therein lies the art and the unadulterated bliss of making a kit your very own.

OK. That's enough with the general introductions. Without further ado, let's giddy-up and get something done!

Charm School 101

WHAT'S SO CHARMING?

A Paean to Our Forebears: Throwing Things onto Flat Surfaces

This much we know: As long as there have been dear hearts on this earth with troubles, burning questions, and a nose for other people's business, there's been a *mancy* (divination) and a *mancer* (diviner) to channel healing, answers, and guidance. For centuries cards and tea leaves have been read, clouds scried, candle wax poured into water, apple stems twisted, lengths of cigarette ash scrutinized, and dice, stalks, and bones thrown.

Long before the advent of the kitchen junk drawer and Cracker Jack prizes, shamans, healers, seers, and the devoutly curious would cast and read bones, shells, stones, and nuts. Unlike the quirky sets that we'll be using, these sacred oracles were mostly drawn from nature's energetic bounty and cast onto natural surfaces: animal hides, dirt, sand, or stone worked admirably. It was held that where and how these pieces landed could reveal great insight into the human condition and our eternal selves. Life's mysteries were explored, and the energetic veil between the living and the dead deferentially parted. The practice of bone reading is made sacred by a connection and veneration of ancestral spirits, as well as a deep respect for plants and animals.

It's both customary and courteous to begin a book on divination with some historical context, its folk roots, origins, and of course, a reverential nod to its pioneers and modern-day practitioners of the ancient methods. This is mine. It's meant less as an academic resource and more as a paean to our forebears. Deep reverence is given to those shamanic tools and practices, and I take this opportunity to celebrate the great Spirit-led work they do.

Just as you'll resonate and attune with one tool or system over another, each individual piece in your kit—its feel, size, color, texture, or quality—will either arouse your intuitive response or shut it down. That's a whole journey in itself. If right off the hop you're drawn to divining with a predominantly organic set, then this shindig might not be for you. We'll be casting with a handmade, more populist, trash-or-treasure, junk-drawer oracle—a meaningful but affable array of knickknackery.

So . . . is it OK that we've strayed from throwing an anointed mink jaw on a grass mat to casting a plastic flamingo on a hankie?

What bedevilment is this?

And while we're on the subject of divining with items typically found jangling on the end of a bracelet or key chain . . . do resin, plastic, glass, ceramic, metallic, or other man-made trinkets have any magical merit?

Well, of course they do.

Everything, whether it's a chestnut or a shower curtain hook, has a unique vibration. Moreover, from the minute you cup a piece in your hands, set an intention for its meaning, or begin the dialogue that asks your charm, *So what do you want to be when you grow up?* it's already being imbued with an energetic imprint. Piece by charmed piece, each trinket, trifle, bauble, and bit will add its own personality to your efforts, the energetic sum of which will be powerful and palpable because it's being informed by you—dear, sweet *magical you!* Admittedly, this won't be a one-way conversation. Your charms will also let you know how they're doing. Sometimes, they'll *'splain* something you've never considered before, which is also how your charms grow vibrationally.

All this aside, precious gems they're not—but jewelry charms have their own illustrious history. They were worn as amulets to ward off evil and as symbols of status or faith. Queen Victoria, Grace Kelly, and Elizabeth Taylor, to name a very few, were practically charm bracelet influencers. Everybody had to have one.

And where are these fabulous collections now? If you have one or can find one of these in a local antique or thrift store, well done you! Unlike other jewelry, someone curates a charm bracelet: it's a menagerie of memories, special days, vacations, people, beliefs, experiences, hopes, and dreams. In much the same way, a button from your grandfather's sweater or your aunt's metal hair curler from the 1950s—and all human-made objects—arrive with their own personal stories. And this is class A energy. Give them loving direction. Show them their stage, and they'll reward you with a command performance time and time again.

You Know You're a Charm Caster When . . . Five Top Signs

You eyeball something shiny, sparkly, or odd, and your inner corvid awakens.

You, as a kid, had a beat-up tin full of marbles, rocks, gumballs, pinata prizes, jacks, and a penny that almost derailed a train.

You get mighty urges to buy things you don't need—(more) tea, chocolate, or cigars—because you want, no *need*, the cool container. Anything to keep the Wee Ones cozy and snug for those few hours when they're not in use. (As we all know, charm casting is a jealous mistress.)

You once glided around the house with a book on your head. Shoulders back, spine straight, eyes on the horizon, perfect posture. You were the model of confidence and grace. Now you meander with your head down and eyes fixed firmly in the dirt and sand. Why wouldn't you? There could be buried treasure underfoot. Shells, stones, bottle caps, bolts, and rubble don't grow on trees. (They didn't teach you that in finishing school.)

Sadly, there's also this:

You impulsively filch dice, tokens, plastic people, and their little castable murder weapons from friends' and family's board games. See Prayer for Forgiveness.

Prayer for Forgiveness

The gambit's lost without the queen,
N42 will n'er be seen.
I'd pass the pigs for you to roll,
But they've been herded to my bowl.

I took the key but left the ring.
On second thought, I need that thing.
No house will land on Baltic Ave.
Forgive my sins, I know, my bad.

Our Beloved Dead and Spirit Helpers: Thank You

Ages ago, when I first began reading for others, usually at a party, I'd find a quiet space, bring out the cards and, you know, foretell. *Wow,* exclaimed my sitters. *How did you know all that?* they'd ask. *Geez,* I'd think, *I must just be so darned clever. I think my grandmother and aunt must have been darned clever too. We're just all so good at knowing stuff.*

Bless my heart, and forgive my folly.

Then that tidal aha broke on the shores of my consciousness. *Oops. I'm just the messenger:* a faithful drudge for the divine—deferential, self-effacing, and perfectly imperfect. When we answer the call to step into service and commit to becoming the clearest channel for Spirit, we get help—a lot of help. There by the grace of our beloved and enlightened ancestors, spirit guides, and helping angels go we. Whether we're on a journey of self-discovery or divining messages for our sitters, they're always there and always have been. By and large, it can be a thankless job, but they never complain. If you just ask, they'll step forward to help you help yourself and others by filling your inner sight, hearing, feeling, and knowing with numinous information.

Our part of the bargain is to stay as open, balanced, and grounded as possible to receive, interpret, then deliver the message with the least amount of energetic distortion. That's also why it's important, as an on-call diviner, to always strive to thrive: Love and work on yourself physically, mentally, and emotionally; keep your vibration high; and be the boss of your own energy. Slowly and graciously strengthening your relationship and connection to your helping spirits will mitigate any uncertainty and elevate your work to new, radiant heights.

Light a candle in the name of Spirit. May power, protection, and the highest vibration of love descend upon your sacred space and all those who enter therein. Call upon your guides and your helpers to assist you in your work. Ask to be the clearest and calmest channel for messages that are helpful, healing, and filled with blessings for all concerned. Align yourself with the light. Let love be the law. Give thanks. And it is so.

Your personal prayer evolves with you. As you learn more about your gifts, spirit team, and work, the words become purer and more profoundly felt and understood, and your petition finds its ideal expression.

> *Neither snow nor rain nor heat nor gloom of night shall keep these couriers from the swift completion of their appointed rounds.*
>
> —The postman's motto

GRIMOIRE PROMPT

Pen a prayer that venerates your ancestors, guides, and helpers and protects your sacred space.

The *Ab Ovo Usque ad Mala* Method: Feasting Romans and Other Madness

When it comes to learning how to begin assigning meanings to your charms, there are many different approaches. I'll be encouraging you to think outside of the charm bag. How? Well . . . *erm* . . . by boldly applying the *ab ovo usque ad mala* method of working and imprinting with your charms.

The ab ovo . . . Say what?

Ab ovo usque ad mala means "from the egg to the apples" or "from beginning to end"—the whole enchilada. Eggs were the food that the Romans served at the beginning of their epic feasting, and then apples came during the last course (right before the food coma). The more common expression is *from soup to nuts*, but who doesn't love a dead language like Latin to inspire a frisson of drama and dark delight? That said, there's also a subtle method to this madness. Every idiom and new bit of knowledge that crosses your path—no matter how obscure and how ab ovo blah-di-blah—every life experience, synchronicity, or random piece of trivia that finds its way into your consciousness will help illuminate brand-new facets of meaning in these seemingly inanimate objects.

So, with these feasting Romans in mind, what new layers of interpretation could be applied to a simple egg, apple, or nut charm? The possibilities are mind-scrambling.

2

The Theory of Every Tiny Thing

Charmspeak: The Divine Language of Trinkets, Trifles, Baubles, and Bits

Kitsch casting with all of its twinkly, sparkly bits is divination's Yellow Brick Road compared to an earthier path. Still, both methods lead to the same sacred destination: an oracular message. We ask that our messages be some, or all, of the following: clear, accurate, clarifying, challenging, enlightening, useful, healing, activating, predictive, revelatory, and insightful. And for Spirit to help you consistently get it right, you'll need to share an understanding. It's a gentle exchange that works something like this: *When I ask you this, you show me that; when you show me that, I'll understand this.* This dialogue is ever-evolving, but begins by opening a new, subtler way of communicating. Learn the syntax of symbols, and you'll become fluent in the divine language of trinkets, trifles, baubles, and bits.

Symbols act like placeholders for words. They represent many things: ideas, ideals, beliefs, identity, locations, people, memories, wounding, or trauma. When events or life experiences are inaccessible, distant, or too hard to face, they can become trapped in our psyche and physical body. They cloud reason and dodge the searchlight. Words won't form. Still there, mind you, they're just playing hooky, floating on a blow-up swan in a pool of avoidance. Symbols have the power to liberate language and unlock doors. They can open dialogues with our unconscious, Highest Good, and Spirit. And once you twig that you're amassing a crack team of totems, you can't help but realize the raw and infinite potential of your casting charms.

Base Kit Basics

Your goal in the hunting and gathering stage—finding or refining pieces for a kit—will be to build a vocabulary. In a casting, think of each charm as a word or words with a job. Every piece has the ability to be a person or thing (noun), an action (verb), or descriptor (adjective or adverb). You'll want an all-purpose set of charms that can answer every question and speak expressively on all subjects. There's nothing like trotting them out, standing back, and feeling your heart swell with pride at their storytelling ability. If you're system has holes, you can naturally rely on your intuitive and psychic ability to fill in gaps and guide you to a message . . . And you could just as easily read a 78-card tarot deck missing a queen and the hanged guy, but would you want to?

In the beginning, it's all about just getting a base kit up and running. Eventually, a more context and narrative-driven approach to refining this set will greatly improve your results.

As an example, say you're divining about the sale of a house. This might seem painfully obvious, but bear with me . . . You'll need, at minimum, charms to represent a house, building, or property; significators for the two "others" of the agent and the buyer; pieces representing a contract or administration; and a red flag that warns, *Don't sign this* or *Find a new agent!* You'll want something to represent yes and no; fast and slow, gain and loss, big and small money. Then after this reading, your base kit will have to stand up to other, completely different contexts, like spirituality, for example: *What does my Highest Good want me to know moving forward?*

If you have superfluous charms that are sucking space and oxygen, you may need to remove them to benefit the collective. There should also be a decent balance between the *yay* (happy face emoji) versus *yikes* (scream emoji) symbols. Here's why: You ask about your BFF's upcoming nuptials and cast the snake, fangs, ring, devil, ax, coffin . . . and bluebird of happiness. Well, there's always the possibility that she's marrying an ax murderer with a bluebird tattoo. But how can you be sure if there's a suspicious lack of auspicious pieces? Balance gives alternative answers a fair shot.

So you see? When crafting a charm kit, it helps to mindfully work backward from all possible questions and answers on the **front end** of the collection process. Here's an exercise designed to put you in touch with your own personal style and warm up the little gray cells.

CASTING GRIMOIRE PROMPT

Write three specific sample questions. Make them open-ended, not the closed-ended yes/no-type questions. This is all hypothetical, so they can be serious or cheeky. For example: *Tell me about my BFF's fiancé?* (Burning, unspoken side question, *What's the diagnosis and prognosis on this marriage?)*

Now imagine, create, and write three different, potential answers for each of these questions, for example:

He's a loyal, hardworking, popular, family guy who loves dogs and will one day become chief of surgery.

He's a penny-pinching, self-involved bore with internet secrets and body odor.

He's a serial ax murderer who loves birds.

Create a checklist. Break down each of your answers into the key charged words you would expect a charm to represent in the interpretation. Ensure that your list includes the main characters (significators, primary, and all others), characteristics, actions, professions, or even emotions. For example:

- BFF
- fiancé
- stranger danger; beware
- falsehearted
- sharp object
- charismatic
- odor
- popular
- secret
- hiding
- a lie
- love
- sadness
- happiness
- loyalty
- surgery
- narcissist
- family
- money
- miser
- internet
- success

If you already have a set of charms, go through it and locate the piece that best represents each of these words and ideas. How is this piece perfect? If not, what's off? Is there a better alternative, but competition for the use of that piece? In other words, are pieces having to perform double duty? Is there a case for adding a new charm or two? If you prefer the less-is-more approach, carry on. I mean, really, what kind of scoundrel would I be to encourage charm hoarding?

The very act of going through this exercise not only solidifies your charms in your own mind, but also communicates to Spirit how you think, receive, and interpret. *When I ask you this, you show me that; when you show me that, I'll interpret this.* And you're already invoking your unique and irrepressible spirit of creativity and play.

> *It is a capital mistake to theorize before one has data.*
> *Insensibly, one begins to twist facts to suit theories,*
> *instead of theories to suit facts.*
> —Sherlock Holmes in *A Scandal in Bohemia*

When you're done journaling, repeat after me: *this exercise is for entertainment purposes only.* We private third eyes know that during an actual divination, you would *never* entertain predetermined answers. As seers, we become specialists in reserving judgment and remaining wide-open to any and all downloads.

Does Size Matter?

How big should your objects be, ideally? They'll come in all shapes and sizes from 10 mm to 45! If you're building your first base kit, it really doesn't matter. Just git 'er done! However, these are my recommendations moving forward—the result of my own tempestuous trials and tribulations, but by no means a hard-and-fast rule. Listen to this cranky author for a few moments, then either applaud or give her a resounding raspberry.

Here are a few things to consider:

You'll want your kits to be comprised of pieces that are more or less the same size. By all means, go chunky if it feels right. Or keep it lighter, more agile. Just try to stay consistent. A notably wonky set will begin to feel unbalanced; the smaller pieces will settle to the bottom of their container like tea dust. And this, unconsciously, can affect the casting process.

First of all, when rifling through your container with eyes closed, your fingers could develop their own tactile agenda—best-catch thinking. Why choose that measly little blob (buddha head) when there's this glorious big thing (long-stemmed rose)? It can—I predict, *will*— bug you over time. Your 26 mm charm will visually pull focus from or overwhelm a 13 mm piece on the casting surface. You don't want it to startle you out of a soft gaze or assume a skewed significance. You're the only one who can come to this conclusion and make the necessary adjustments.

All that posited, there's a time, place, and heightened role for those special, slightly larger look-at-me pieces, such as in a Very Important Pieces set, and we'll explore this in detail later (see VIPs, page 21).

To 3D or Not to 3D: A Good Question

When I first started, my casting kits were amazing, don't get me wrong—but basic. They were mostly comprised of one-sided metal or zinc alloy charms. I'd turn over the 2D car charm and it looked like it had driven through 100 miles of bad road—and possibly over that flat wedding cake. In a pro/con list for this type of charm, a pro is that you'll instantly see if the charm is presenting right side up or reversed (RX); a con is that depending on how it's landed or what's piled up on top of it, a featureless flip side always makes identification a pain in the charm arsenal. To see what it is, you may have to get in there with your sharp pointer and flip it, and possibly other charms, over. It's a speed bump.

The happy news is that these days it's much easier to find really well-crafted 3D charms, some of which even have moving parts that open and close or splay like fish on a fishing rod or playing card aces. When reversed, the back of a 3D charm is far more detailed. Advantage? You'll be able to tell a reversed buddha from a gorilla—always a good thing. Naturally, this falls into the arena of personal style and the inherent needs of the adherent. Is flat and no-frills fine? Or are you warming to the idea of a few 3Ds with extra personality that pop? Regardless, you can sleep on it: your forever set is a labor of love and a work-in-perpetual-progress.

Dos and Don'ts: Leave These Alone!

Fragile or glass: I've had, despite knowing better, many potentially breakable pieces in my kits and, over time, they've fulfilled their prophecy, to wit: the beautiful, I-just-need-to-have mini gemstone mushrooms. They've all brought back the horror of Marie Antoinette: caps severed from their stems! Know that if something can break, it will. It's another reason why it helps to refine your technique and also balance your kit not only in size, but maybe also in weight lest the more delicate pieces get T-boned. Your charms need to be toss-able, able to hold their own against any others that, based on composition, are indestructible and have invincibility on their sides.

> *"Well! I've often seen a cat without a grin,"*
> thought Alice; *"but a grin without a cat!*
> *It's the most curious thing I ever saw in all my life!"*
> —Lewis Carroll, *Alice's Adventures in Wonderland*

Scribble

If a piece gets damaged, before throwing it away consider working it into a new version of itself. Take, for instance, those mushroom caps and stems. The mushroom, because it thrives in dark, damp places, is my symbol for something that incubates in darkness—a secret. (How you resonate with this symbol might be completely different.) Working with this scenario for the moment, how might you assign separate meanings for the broken cap and stem pieces?

You may be thinking, I don't have any breakable pieces, so why do I need to get all forensic about a mushroom? Contemplating the anatomy of any of your pieces can give you a more layered and detailed interpretation when other charms touch, kiss, oppose, kick, bite, smother, hug, or block these specific areas.

Let's say that you have a runner charm and a telescope lands across its leg or foot. The meaning of your charm remains intact, but that one area now feels extra relevant or, in charmspeak, charged. What's a telescope? What does it do? It's a device used to see things in the distance. What's this thing in the distance? A goal? Land—a destination? If the whole runner embodies an act of rapid physical movement, what's the role of the leg or foot? A key step, perhaps. That top charm blocks or restrains the energy of the one on the bottom. So something's asking you to slow down a sec and look more closely at one aspect of the goal. Now what if the telescope had landed across the runner's head, completely obscuring its vision? What might this be saying about the goal itself or the planner moving forward?

Sharp or round: You shouldn't ever need to have a tetanus shot before handling your charms. If it can cut, stab, or puncture, think again. You don't want to learn the hard way. It's not easy to resist including that century-old rusted nail or shard of thick glass from the candle that exploded the day your favorite rock star died, but: NO. It's best to note whatever message that original item imparted and then find a fitting replacement—or file it down. As for round things: they roll . . . and roll . . . and bounce. You're charm casting, not playing pinball.

Heirloom: Oh, the energetic imprint! The history! The expense? It's up to you, but remember, casting pieces can by nature be wild at heart and transient. They like to jump. Some seek freedom. If you can't bear losing this piece, don't include it in your casting set.

Whatsits, whosits, and thingamabobs: If you don't know what it is or frankly what it's doing there, put it in a nice jar, revisit it, and assign a meaning later. While it's tempting to just randomly add eye-catching pieces to your kit, it's not so great when they show up during a casting and you're like—*OMG, what's this*? First of all, it will knock you out of your soft gaze and throw you into your rational mind where the monkeys live. Second, you'll be shooting barrels in a fish. Don't do it.

The General Reading: Life Areas

You or your sitter, main significator, querent—the one asking the questions—wants their "fortune" told. There are decisions to make and directions to take; something big and vague wants to be broken down in digestible pieces. Then, there'll be the "Que Sera, Sera" queries requiring prowess in the predictive arts: *Will I be rich? What lies ahead?. . . Will I marry? Will I have a tolerable job?* You get the point. These are the types of questions, both eternal and infernal, at the heart and soul of every forecasting. Not only will you have to divine answers and wisdom for these, but undoubtably also answer questions that haven't even been consciously asked. No rest for the weary!

Meaningful castings, then, must rely on the graceful and constantly shifting choreography between this time-honored pas de deux:

A surface: This is a framework that features general life areas, grand-scheme topics, and universal themes—the experience of being alive.

and

Casting pieces: Your system of symbols that, in combination with these life areas, will provide relevant details; they'll flesh out the narrative.

The VIP (Very Important Pieces) Method: Charms with Extra Clout and Roles

This is a traditional technique with a kitsch caster's twist. It's also where we begin joyriding away from any potential comfort zone. If you're a charm caster who swears by your illustrated casting mats—no worries, come along anyway. You won't need (too much) mad money; just an open mind and definitely a sparkling soda.

For your every convenience, casting mats, maps, charts, or cloths provide a stylized framework for your reading. They've already been divided into key life areas or segments and so instantly establish context for the landed charms. For example, the designer will have chosen a symbol, such as the caduceus for the health and wellness segment, or printed words, such as *finance & means* for the money life area. No guidebook needed. It's easy, effortless, and yes, efficient. When a toilet charm lands in the area of love and romance, you have a good handle on where that relationship is headed.

The VIP (Very Important Pieces) method offers you the option of replacing a fancy casting surface. The VIPs are an additional, compact kit of charms that not only represent all of these life areas and hot topics but, with practice, will also support a more nuanced and cohesive interpretation. Together they're a special task force, first responders who arrive on scene and set the divination in motion. They're look-at-me pieces that want extra or immediate attention. Some seasoned casters have these pieces already incorporated into their main kit. I recommend keeping them in a separate bag for a few reasons.

Here is everything you need to know about VIPs. Come meet the team, see how they roll, and then decide.

VIP pieces, although relatively consistent in size, can be marginally larger than the charms in your main kit. While you'll get to know them intimately, on first gaze it's still helpful to be able to distinguish them from the other base kit charms. Because this set has fewer pieces, you'll have the luxury of being extra picky about the individual aesthetic, sentimentality, or quality of the objects. This is why I also have a slightly tighter charmventory for these ones.

Since they are kept in a separate container from your main charms, you would randomly select your VIP charms first. How many? Always let your intuition advise your fingers. If there's a number that's significant to the divination, use that. For example, if your question is *what do I need to know about our camping trip to the Allegheny Mountains?* You leave in three days; you're staying for eight days; four of you are going. So whichever of these digits feels charged, select that number of pieces.

Once the VIPs have been selected, you can go ahead and cast them. Then select and cast your base kit charms around the VIPs, just as you would sprinkle them over a graphically designed mat or cloth. You can also preselect a VIP to establish the context for a specific casting. Place it into the middle of a bracelet or surface, and cast around it. As this piece represents what is consciously known, select one or two more to divine the unknown factors that deepen your understanding.

Personally, I don't like to see my charms before they're all cast. Maybe you're like this too. It's the same as leaving cards face down until I'm ready to divine. Why? Because the minute my brain becomes aware of incoming stimuli, the monkeys begin to jump around and chatter. And I'm the one doing the reading, thank you very much—not them. So I keep a small *blind* bowl to the side of my cloth to hold the mix of my randomly selected VIPs and base kit charms prior to casting. I can't see them—nor can the monkeys.

VIPs are perfect for daily, small space, or remote general readings. Ask: *What do I need to know about my day*? Place a bracelet in the middle of a solid-color 12-by-12 handkerchief. Randomly select a VIP or two and a few charms and interpret your message. Nothing could be finer—or simpler.

In a larger general casting, find your VIP pieces first. They'll get the party started. They'll carry the first, foundational layer of meaning: the framework or theme of the casting. At times, the synthesis of these pieces alone holds the actual answer. Before you cast, you can even ask Spirit for a specific VIP to present to validate something.

If you're doing a general reading and the finance piece shows up, you're obviously going to read for that life area. But what if you've asked a specific question regarding finances and that piece doesn't land? It's all good. When the context is already understood, there's often no reason for that piece to stand up. It simply makes room for its castmates to add their voice into the mix. For instance, you've asked about finances. The VIP **self-care** piece shows up. It's flanked by the base kit charms **adding machine** and **vampire bat**. Are your finances being drained (vampire bat) by the hot yoga studio *plus* retail therapy *plus* the pumpkin spice frappuccino fix? What if, the finance piece—one out of thirty charms—presents? Feel that increase in urgency? This really wants to drive home a point.

Life Areas/Hot Topics Kit: Pros in a Nutshell

- You're in the driver's seat. You get to choose your own symbols, apply your own language and imaginings. You're always in control of the framework for your own casting—its size, system, and structure.
- Working on a quieter, less visually distracting space allows you to become more sensitive to energy. Opening your clairaudient, clairsentient, and

claircognizant channels lets you hear, feel, or just know what your charms are there to convey.

- It's a smaller kit. Remember that fabulous container that your current collection has grown out of? Well, you can use it again. Oh, and did I mention that now you'll have a sound excuse for playing with more charms? It's a win, win.

One Slightly Annoying Thing about VIPs

If you decide to keep your VIPs in a separate container, once your casting is finished, get into the sanity-saving habit of putting them back into their bag ASAP before clearing off the other pieces. Otherwise you'll be fishing through your other charms, watching time slip through your hands. Don't worry. You'll get used to this—because you'll have to.

Games, Chains, Drawers, and Floors

TRINKET-RICH ENVIRONMENTS

As mentioned earlier, you can easily get starter charm kits online. If, however, you want to gather cool pieces without breaking the bank or you find thrill in the hunt, serendipity, and synchronicity, beat a path to the following locations.

Yo-Ho-Ho: Pillaging for Pieces

Monopoly? Clue? Casters find board games irresistible. So much so that you'll need to apply great self-discipline to leave the pawns in the box. You can often find used games at garage and yard sales, flea markets, antique and thrift stores: the originals as well as variations on the classic theme—the quirkier the better. Pewter Cat and Dog-opoly tokens such as the steak, Spike dog bowl, sardine and cat food tin pawns make adorable additions or swap-out pieces. Hope the ball isn't missing a jack or two; mini four- and three-spot tiles have also been known to disappear from dominoes. Traditionally, this tile right side up means luck; reversed—well, not so much. White and black Go stones can make definitive yes and no pieces. You can also search eBay or other online sites for game replacement tokens. (Evidently sticky-fingered casters are more common than we think!) Go forth, me hearty! Ransack and rummage! But if you need to keep your conscience clean, revisit the Prayer for Forgiveness (page 10).

Chains (Cords and Ceiling Fans)

Buying a cheap mini (jewelry) plier set is a sound investment. The tiny round nose, chain nose, and side cutter prove very helpful when taking apart necklaces, bracelets, earrings, key chains, and ceiling fan and zipper pulls. My motto? If it sits attractively on a chain or a cord, imagine what it will look like in your charm kit. Cutter in hand, nothing's safe.

Let's be honest. There's a lot of questionable costume jewelry out there. Pure vintage eyesore. Luckily, pliers in hand, you can get an upcycling and salvage operation underway. Isolate the best beads or charms—those diamonds in the rough—and find the beauty in the butt-ugly. Snip, liberate, and commandeer those pieces into service. You wouldn't be caught dead wearing that frog toggle on a cowboy hat around your neck, but charm casting? Hell yeah! And don't forget to keep a jar filled with interesting beads for your DIY casting mala (see page 73).

Space (or taste)-conscious people rarely hang on to gifted or inherited imitation jewelry. Therefore and thankfully, secondhand vendors are a great source for individual pieces or bag o' crap-style collections. Repurposing always does our planet and hearts a world of good. Supporting your local charity shops contributes to a good cause, and you still walk away feeling like a bandit. One person's trash is clearly the caster's treasure.

Drawers (Or Attics, Basements, Pockets, Boxes, and Bags)

Just that word: *drawer.* All dark, secretive, shambolic—it instantly arouses curiosity and a longing to rifle through things hidden, forgotten, forbidden, taboo, buried, or squirreled. At least that's an accurate description of my drawers. Maybe you're the organized kind: an über-Virgo whose socks are folded into origami. *I think I'll wear the striped crane today, or maybe the jacquard swan.* Regardless of your domestic principles, there's usually at least one nihilist nook in every residence. The kitsch caster's kryptonite is truly the kitchen *junk drawer*.

I've heard declutter and downsizing professionals try and rebrand these as *utility drawers*. Why? Because, heaven forfend, who wants small, junky things in our gracious homes? They're not wrong: We don't. We want them in our casting kits. And yet, dear Diviner, don't think of your drop zones as personal dumpsters, but rather see them as safe havens for estranged items. A mini carabiner, Phillips bit from a micro screwdriver, zipper, paper clip, coins, buttons, coated hair band—these small odds and sods shall soon mix and mingle with other pieces and become a handmade oracle.

Here are some other micro universes that have hopefully been kept safe from compulsive reorganization. Best check out some of these, too:

- Sewing and jewelry boxes
- Tool kits
- Dollhouses
- Storage lockers
- Garage, shed, basement or outbuilding cabinets
- Old handbags or suitcases

Floors (And Down Where the Goblins Go, Below, Below, Below . . .)

I spy with my third eye, something that is . . . Even if, like me, you weren't great at science, thanks to Isaac Newton and his gravitational theories, we all know that stuff falls to the ground. Big stuff gets cleared sooner because it's a slip and fall hazard. (I figured this out myself.) Tiny things, however, sometimes get overlooked because Spirit knows casters are coming.

It helps to pay attention. When in cahoots with the Wee Ones, you'd be surprised at what begins to appear along your path. Spirit can and will redirect your focus to a piece that's waiting where you'd least expect it on a floor, shelf, or bench, in the sand and dirt—or underneath a radiator. When you're bestowed a piece, it's nice to give thanks. And it's good to let the universe know that your eyes are wide-open. You're following that hunch—and leaving no sofa cushion unturned.

Exotic Environments

Whenever you're out of your area code, dedicate some time to nosing around the shops. I've found really amazing pieces in hospital and museum gift stores and the kind of eclectic establishments that sell soap, candles, and things that soothe broken dreams.

People, Murders, and Unkindnesses

Years ago, I was told matter-of-factly that people will start bringing you things.

"People give me charms all the time."

C'mon, I snorted in disbelief.

As it turns out, it's true. It's one thing that you've been bitten by the baubles and bits bug, but quite another to watch friends and family view castoffs through a new lens. Instead of walking past or discarding them, they'll pocket these pieces for you—just in case. I've been given buttons, cuff links, coins (one that even took a bullet), a tiny bubble level, and lots of this and that. Trust me: turn on that beacon.

Then there's this phenomenon. If you're blessed enough to have a murder of crows or an unkindness (I prefer flock) of ravens hanging out in your backyard, feed them peanuts and quail's eggs. Make them feel safe. Intelligent, highly aware, and psychic, these birds have been known to repay the kindness by leaving an assortment of sticks, stones, toy cars, buttons, and jewelry for you.

Nothing fosters belief better than results. Write down a piece that you would love to manifest. Trust that it's out there somewhere, looking for you too. When it shows up, full of magic and ready to tumble, give thanks and celebrate the event with a sticker and a date.

Come to me: ____________________________

☐ **Date:** ____________________________

Always make the search as much fun as the discovery

Places to go. Pieces to see.

Let the Wee Ones know you're coming. Set your intention to find special pieces. Make your dream list of places to visit and, flashlight in hand, spaces to explore:

Hunting and Gathering: Find These

Remember the days when you came back home from trick-or-treating, then emptied your bag to inspect the bounty? This is what a charm haul feels like: *Booyah!* But unavoidably, now it's time to turn it all into a workable system. Remember, the end goal of building any kit is to find the right mix of pieces that give balance, versatility, and scope. It takes time, nips, tucks, and tweaks to get it *right*—if there is such a thing. But while you're having a blast honing your forever system, keeping and amending a master checklist of charms will help you stay on top of what you've got and what you still need. In this section, I'll give you an example of a tried-and-true kit and casting system, a blend of some traditional but mostly kitsch elements—and a few starter meanings. Take what resonates or make those changes that make intuitive sense to *you*. But first, let's review this VIP and Base Kits approach.

Life Areas vs. Hot Topics: What's the Diff?

Life areas are the big asks, the most popular and general contexts for divination. Now we can take these life areas and break them down into subcategories: **hot topics**. For example, wellness can be blown out into diet, exercise, healing, recovery, grounding, and meditation. Your VIP kit can be very basic—just the key life areas—but adding a few more specific hot topics pieces gives you a more nuanced reading and a higher degree of certainty.

The VIP Kit: A Basic Checklist

- ☐ People:
    - ☐ main significator—Self
    - ☐ secondary significator—Other, partner, significant second party
    - ☐ third-party significator—family, friend, acquaintance, colleague, known or unknown

- ☐ Soul, purpose, alignment, eternal self
- ☐ Spirit, source, Highest Good, messenger of light, energetic flow
- ☐ Love, romance, relationships
- ☐ Commitments, partnerships, union, contracts
- ☐ Home, close, local away
- ☐ Away—far, distance, someone else's home
- ☐ Money, means, resources
- ☐ Health, wellness
- ☐ Spirituality, faith
- ☐ Career, vocation, business
- ☐ Education, academia, training, teaching, lessons and learning
- ☐ Art, beauty, creativity, enterprise
- ☐ Family
- ☐ Friends, social life, recreation, hobbies
- ☐ Travel
- ☐ Beginning
- ☐ Ending
- ☐ Memento mori—symbolic, *remember you must die*—so carpe diem. Be present. Live each day like it was your last.

Your turn. Take a few of these life areas and break them down into subcategories, or hot topics.

Need It. Got It. Got It. Need It: The Base Kit Checklists

There's no hurry. Take as long as you need to find or attract your pieces. If you're new to the casting arts, then think of this as a scavenger hunt. *Off you go. Godspeed. Remember to hydrate.*

I'm always blown away by my fellow caster's kits. Even if you already have a bodacious set, I'm hoping that something here might still spark some new ideas.

You'll soon notice that there's repetition in the following checklists. I have a few intentional duplicates in both my VIP and base kits. While they're not physically the same charm, they carry a similar, if not the exact same meaning. With so many pieces, the chances of the same charm landing twice are slim to none. So when you beat these odds, pay attention. It's one of the many endearing ways that your charms make sure you're awake.

Traditional Pieces and Meanings

- ☐ **(Second) bracelet or chain**—What's inside? What wants you to see it now? Is it twisted? How many times? Once, twice, more? That could indicate there are tangles, complications to be worked out, or multiple steps or stages in a process.
- ☐ **Ring(s)**—partnerships, commitments, relationships, marriage. You can have one ring for a heavy, unwanted commitment and another for a light, easy, or easy to get out of commitment.
- ☐ **Bell**—heads-up, important in the moment, alarm, mayday.
- ☐ **Coin(s)**—Money. Three different coins can tell you how much: small, medium, or lots and lots. These can also mean workplace and boss. Find a coin such as a U.S. penny with a building on one side (workplace) and a face on the other (boss or management).
- ☐ **Seed**—potential, magic bean. Spirit is saying, *go ahead, plant and nurture this.*

- ☐ **Hand(s)**—palm side up, you give or something is taken; palm side down, you take (imagine the fingers drawing something toward you). And a second hand—palm side up, you receive; palm side down, something must be given (imagine pushing something away from you—not the piece you'll want to see come tax time).
- ☐ **Arrow**—directs your focus away, to a specific charm or area. Shows rapid movement.

Scribble

Keep your eyes open for pieces that are bone or stick-like, longer, thinner, or having two different ends, such as a bar, nail, arrow, flowering branch, or doll's leg. They'll carry their own meanings, but also act as a barrier or boundary to separate, block, underscore, point, or be a function of a timeline.

- ☐ **Dice**—(see page 171) the number rolled can establish both the setting and advice for your reading.
- ☐ **Key**—unlocks or locks, a solution
- ☐ **Cowrie shell**—if the teeth are up, it's talking: time to speak; if the teeth are down, it's not talking: time to be quiet; active listening.
- ☐ **Thimble**—work to do, labor. Also, a protective carapace
- ☐ **Cross**—burdens, crosses to bear, tests, trials and tribulations (Alternatively, it can be faith depending on your belief system.)
- ☐ **Button(s)**—attachments, connections, or time to stop talking—button it up. I have a button with a plain and a flowery side. Plain represents the withholding of praise or compliments; flowery warns of flattery.

White and black buttons—auspicious and inauspicious attachments or connections.

- ☐ **Skull(s)**—ancestors, ancestral patterns or traits. Two separate colors can distinguish between the maternal and paternal lines; a light skull can indicate a known ancestor and a black one, an unknown ancestor farther back on the family tree.
- ☐ **Domino**—a piece where the numbers add to seven is lucky; reversed, blank, unlucky; reversed can represent a coffin or a grave.
- ☐ **Elephant** (trunk up)—pushing through obstacles

My Coolest Charm

FROZEN CHARLOTTE OR A CORPSE GOING TO A BALL

My coolest charm is based on the macabre Victorian tale of a vain girl heading to a ball in frightfully frosty weather. Her mother begged her to cover herself with a blanket, but she wanted her dress to be seen, and also not attend smelling like a horse. Upon her arrival at the ball, they pulled her frozen, lifeless, pale but vain body from the sleigh. It's easy to see how this doll charm can represent willfulness and the disastrous consequence of shrugging off sound advice. (The metal versions are better for casting as opposed to ceramic—or you'll have a broken Charlotte).

Base Kit Charms

PEOPLE

- ☐ **Main significator**—self, the *you*, personality, persona. Whenever it lands, you're being called "to the mat." Have fun with this piece. Make it personal.
- ☐ **Secondary significator**—other, partner, significant second party relevant to this reading
- ☐ **Known person**—third-party family, friend, acquaintance, colleague
- ☐ **Unknown person**—third-party stranger, someone you'll meet soon or never meet
- ☐ **Child**—offspring, innocent, childlike, naive, immature, unevolved
- ☐ **Baby**—infant or fertility, newbie
- ☐ **Couple or group**—two or more parties involved, a group or team, teamwork
- ☐ **Friends and kindred spirits**—social life; a friend that has your back

---

Scribble

When finding charms, work with pieces that resonate personally. Lenormand readers might cast a dog into the role of friendship. But if your bestie gave you a gumball-machine troll when you were twelve, it already carries that imprint of friendship—so that's your piece. Check it off.

- ☐ **Devil**—false friend, trickster, temptation, enemy, traitor, interfering party, malicious, narcissistic, bad intentions
- ☐ **Helping hand**—assistance, support system, network, charity, volunteering
- ☐ **Family**—kin, and sometimes kith
- ☐ **Ancestor**—a transitioned loved one
- ☐ **Family tree**—ancestry, lineage, origin
- ☐ **Tutelary**—spirit guides/helping spirits, angels, animal totems
- ☐ **True north**—alignment, soul purpose and potential
- ☐ **Home**—Use the reverse side to mean *away.*
- ☐ **Birdhouse**—sanctuary, a place or space where you feel free to be you
- ☐ **Institution(s)**—authority, official, government, hospital, jail, university, church
- ☐ **Technology**—computers, internet, social media
- ☐ **Love**—romance, emotions, affairs of the heart, heart chakra
- ☐ **Black heart**—evil, sociopathy, bitterness, resentment
- ☐ **Changeable heart**—fickle, the heart's changed its' mind
- ☐ **Heartbreak**—deep emotional stress
- ☐ **Passion**—will, ambition, goals, sex, ego-driven desire, solar plexus chakra
- ☐ **Temptation**—inner demons, addictions, lures of the baser instincts
- ☐ **Tradition**—conventions, the mainstream, customs
- ☐ **Revolution**—defiance, anger, unconventionality, reform
- ☐ **Change**—transformation, transition for better or for worse
- ☐ **Chance**—risk-taking, gambling, lottery

- ☐ **Sunlight, day**—conscious mind, awareness, confidence, revelation, success, improvement, energy
- ☐ **Moonlight, night**—ebb and flow, phases, illusion, madness
- ☐ **Starlight**—clarity, hope, guidance, direction, individuality, self-actualization, fame
- ☐ **Unconscious**—hidden drivers, motivation, unprocessed or unintegrated experience, projections
- ☐ **Secrets**—hidden, unrevealed, mask, under the radar
- ☐ **Truth**—trustworthy, honest, transparent
- ☐ **Lie**—deception, manipulation, gaslighting
- ☐ **Eye**—look here, closer, deeper; examination, investigation
- ☐ **Spiritual protection**—spiritual crisis, the existence of or need for protection, cracks in the auric armor
- ☐ **Physical protection**—warning against theft or other nonspiritual threats, boundaries; watch your back, assets, and body; manage your energy
- ☐ **Self-love**—self-care, me-time
- ☐ **Self-esteem**—value, worth, self-perception, inner goddess
- ☐ **Mind**—intellect, psychology, wit
- ☐ **Body**—our physical container
- ☐ **Spirit**—Highest Good, incarnation, source, crown chakra
- ☐ **Coin**—a little bit of money
- ☐ **Coin**—a medium amount of money
- ☐ **Coin**—a great deal of money

- ☐ **Yes**—affirmative, go
- ☐ **No**—negative, stop
- ☐ **Past**
- ☐ **Present**
- ☐ **Future**
- ☐ **Old**—advanced age, elder, established, antique
- ☐ **New**—beginning, scion, growth
- ☐ **Endings**—death, as in there's no going back, decay
- ☐ **Short**—short-lived, short time, transient, here today, gone tomorrow
- ☐ **Long**—enduring, standing the test of time
- ☐ **Fast**—timing: now, yesterday; lightning bolt, sudden, out-of-the-blue, surprise
- ☐ **Slow**—painstaking pace; timing: don't hold your breath. Perseverance and patience required.
- ☐ **Sharp**—sever this! Danger, insolvability, surgery, mastery with sharp objects
- ☐ **Tool**—building, construction, repair, tear down, renovation
- ☐ **Opportunity**—receptivity, open doors, improvement
- ☐ **Creativity**—artistic, expressive, unique and resourceful
- ☐ **Science**—scientist, rational and evidence-based thinking or approach
- ☐ **Fertility**—sensuality, conception of both new life and ideas, sacral chakra
- ☐ **Beauty**—aesthetics; a love, need, or appreciation of that which uplifts and inspires; romanticizing your life; someone or something attractive
- ☐ **Medical**—doctor, nurse, formal medicine and practitioners

- ☐ **Wellness**—well-being, alternative medicine and practitioners, midwifery, diet, nutrition, supplements
- ☐ **DNA**—predispositions, epigenetic markers, genetic origins, what makes you distinctly unique
- ☐ **Emergency**—injury, unfortunate event, emergency services
- ☐ **Cure**—antidote (I use a whole nutmeg as it was historically known as a cure-all.)
- ☐ **Loyalty**—allegiance, trustworthiness
- ☐ **Laughter**—funny, joyful; you'll be laughing soon.
- ☐ **Tears**—sadness, grief, wounding; you'll be crying soon.
- ☐ **Writing**—pen to paper; scribe, journalist, or author; written correspondence
- ☐ **Communication**—conversation, throat chakra
- ☐ **Gossip**—talking smack behind one's back, negative self-chatter, an earful
- ☐ **Reputation**—how one's perceived, recognized, and appreciated; image, fame
- ☐ **Status quo**—same old, pattern, lack of challenge, conventional, traditional
- ☐ **Trinity**—three connected things, the sum being greater than the individual parts, a third and separate energy that two parts create
- ☐ **Stability**—anchor, safe, secure, strength, rooted
- ☐ **Decision**—a choice already or about to be made
- ☐ **Cause and effect**—actions and choices leading to a consequence, responsibility, accountability
- ☐ **Education**— school, academia, training, teaching, lessons and learning, online courses

- ☐ **Pattern**—here we go again; comfort zone; repetition of thoughts, emotions, acts, or behavior
- ☐ **Stuck**—stagnation; lack of motivation, movement, or progress
- ☐ **AHA**—a bright idea, epiphany, breakthrough, pattern-breaker
- ☐ **Evolution**—enlightenment, progress, spiritual growth and ascension
- ☐ **Lessons**—academic or spiritual tests and initiations
- ☐ **Power and empowerment**—power broker, authority, dominance, inner sovereignty, duty, discipline, personal sacrifice, leadership, ruling in your own right. *Reversed:* abuse of authority, imbalance, dictatorship
- ☐ **Diva**—a peacock, stepping into a spotlight or one's radiance with an unshakable sense of self and style, self-made success. *Reversed:* attention-seeking, high maintenance, temperamental
- ☐ **Fame**—resounding success, limelight, acknowledgement, accolades, star-quality, celebrity
- ☐ **Criminality**—corruption, fraud, violence, abuse, negligence
- ☐ **Self-reflection**—self-image, looking within
- ☐ **Play**—craic

> *Craic* is a fabulous Irish slang word that means having a laugh, a really no-holds-barred time. *What's the craic?* What's the news? What's happening? Good craic involves friends and spirited connections with others, banter, gossip, and hijinks. A craic piece can either herald amusement or remind you not to take yourself or life too seriously.

- ☐ **Conflict and chaos**—frustration, confusion, mild differences or intense clashes; batten down the hatches; an episode or period of clipped wings and restrained will; arguments, fights, violence

- ☐ **Work**—job or career; you work to live
- ☐ **Vocation**—a calling or high-powered profession; you live to work
- ☐ **Busyness**—industriousness, elbow grease
- ☐ **Adventure**—long-distance travel, journey, foreign or unfamiliar, at a distance, risk
- ☐ **Environment**—local surroundings, short trips, something external or out of your control
- ☐ **Weather**—Outside conditions, a state, climate or atmosphere, preparedness, the skill to navigate a challenging event
- ☐ **Magic**—unseen, mystery, the esoteric, occult
- ☐ **Spirituality and faith**—belief system
- ☐ **Warrior**—self-reliance, courage, combating fear or inertia, rising to a challenge
- ☐ **Perception**—something being viewed or experienced through a personal filter
- ☐ **Ice**—winter, something cooling or frozen, rigidity, disconnect
- ☐ **Heat**—summer, hot, temperature rising, escalation
- ☐ **Rest**—autumn, resistance energy, relaxation, rejuvenation
- ☐ **Renewal**—spring, regeneration
- ☐ **Peace**—olive branch, calm, tranquility, harmony, conflict resolution, reunion, rapprochement
- ☐ **Healing**—recovery, shaman, healer
- ☐ **Intuition**—downloads, insight, instinct
- ☐ **Witch**—seer, diviner, wise one, psychic, medium, spiritual practitioner

- ☐ **Gratitude**—thanksgiving, harvest, appreciation and acknowledgment of personal blessings
- ☐ **Wholesome**—clean and slow living
- ☐ **Stillness**—calmness, being present, grounding, root chakra
- ☐ **Wild**—raw, undomesticated, unrefined, nature, camping
- ☐ **Reward**—fruitful, ROI, victory, success, triumph, prize
- ☐ **Luck**—fortune smiles; you make your own. *Reversed:* unlucky; change is an ally.
- ☐ **Gift**—a surprise offering that raises your spirits, compliments or praise
- ☐ **Special occasion**—anniversary, celebration, event
- ☐ **Loss**—deterioration, mess, slow or fast corrosion, theft
- ☐ **Obstacle**—delay, hurdle to overcome, speed bump, blockage, mountain, opposition
- ☐ **Desert**—unfamiliar territory, mirages, arid phase, wasteland, stagnation, effort without recognition, feeling lost, lack of bearings

> *Full many a flower is born to blush unseen*
> *And waste its sweetness on the desert air.*
> —Thomas Gray

- ☐ **Temperance**—balance, avoidance of extremes, moderation, assertive vs. reactive
- ☐ **Mastery**—excellence, skill, meticulous attention to detail; an expert, specialist, mentor

LOOK WHAT I FOUND

Occasionally and as you see fit, why not celebrate and document the story of a special find for posterity in your casting grimoire? (My own example: the butcher's twine.) You may not think so now, but there will be origin stories that you'd wished you'd taken the time to preserve. And sometimes, when you need it most, you can revisit these entries—this ultimate testimony of your magical gifts—and be able to say: *Dang, I really do live a charmed life!*

Date: ______________________________

Piece: ______________________________

Backstory: ______________________________

____

Description: ______________________________

____

Notes: ______________________________

____

____

____

____

____

____

____

Themed Kits

While your base kit can handle pretty much anything you throw at it—and throw it at—some subjects can benefit from a more customized approach. Charms are words, right? So consider that different folks and fields have their own lingo and insider's vocabulary and what's comprehensible to the poker player might not be to an air traffic controller and vice versa. When we build a themed kit, we're cobbling together a communication system that supports and works backward from a theme.

The size of your kits will vary widely, depending on the subject, of course, and how deep you'll want to dive. Need I mention that this puts all of those extra or duplicate charms to very good use? Don't feel guilty. It's widely accepted that casting kits can be like dachshunds or pugs: you can't just have one. Here are a few ideas for companion kits:

- Love, Romance, and Relationships
- Self-Care
- Shadow Work
- Awakening the Creative Self
- Spirituality and Magic
- Animal Communication
- Business, Finance, and Career
- Ancestral Healing
- Sports
- Investigative: True Crime
- Paranormal
- Manifestation
- True North: Purpose and Alignment

The Tour Rider: Your Kit's Special Performance Requirements

I used to work in the music industry. Once, for a big concert promotions company. One of my many glaze-your-eyes-over-with-boredom jobs was to photocopy the artists' contracts, including a special multipage tour rider that outlined, in binding and no uncertain terms, the musicians' requirements—technical and, um, otherwise. Who knew that years later I'd be entertaining the same high-maintenance demands for my themed casting kits.

I like to think of these sets as elite. They've all been selected, trained, and equipped to handle special jobs. They're a lot like rock stars, with their distinctive style, voice, attitude, quirks—and asks. The *A–Z* experience of creating a themed kit from scratch and identifying and catering to the special needs of a context will make you a more versatile caster. Dedicating this kind of attention and you-time to your pieces gives your kit *drivetrain*: the energetic momentum that helps you navigate the terrain of any casting like a headliner.

Hey Google: Life Is But a Theme

I know this will sound like classic overkill, but before you create a custom kit, it helps to do a little research. Take the theme of Love, Romance, and Relationships. It's not all birds and bees, and like any special set, its tour rider has some bold requirements. When I was building mine, I learned that there are different kinds of love: erotic, affectionate, storge or familial (no more sexy time), obsessive, playful, selfless or enduring. And there are also many kinds of relationships: codependent, controlling, held together by loss, toxic, trophy, long-distance, affair, and friends with benefits. Then behold the five love languages: gifts, words of affirmation, quality time, physical touch, acts of service . . . charms. (Evidently there are six . . .) And what about the level and nature of the commitment? Is that secondary significator monogamous and capable of shared support? A caretaker? A scoundrel? A pack animal that prefers the company of friends (or mother)? Needy? Are they all hat and no cattle? Solitary, fragile, and unavailable? One simple heart charm can't say all of this.

Scientia potentia est—knowledge really is power. The more you understand about your context, the more creatively you can recruit charms that will stand up to the zeitgeist.

Love and romance, as one of the diviner's main bread and butter contexts, makes a great themed kit. And there's one type of relationship reading that's becoming more common: friendship. Assessing the fallout from a seemingly mild misunderstanding or tempestuous throwdown will include a backstory. *What happened? What went boom?* Why did the once inseparable besties emerge from the wreckage estranged? The loss of a close friend, by breakup or death, can make you heartsick. In some cases, friends know each other longer or sometimes even better than a romantic partner. *Can it be fixed? Is this a friend for life, a reason, or a season?*

There are always two sides to a story, and you'll want pieces tasked with getting the skinny on all parties, their respective characters, motivations, hopes, fears, beliefs, illusions, attitudes, emotions, limitations, strengths, and resources. Additionally, your kit and system will want to have deep and healing chats about these kinds of things:

- Understanding, processing, and accepting an event
- Prioritizing self-care and self-reflection
- Honoring personal needs including boundaries
- Constructive communication
- Recognizing red flags
- Finding closure and moving on—or repairing, reuniting, and reconnecting
- Attracting *anam cara* (soul friends)—those more kindred in spirit

Animating the Inanimate

Charmatis Personae: Casting Charms in Their Leading Roles

Imagine that your casting surface is a stage in a grand theater. The red velvet curtain is still closed, and the air is electric with anticipation. The candles lining the front of the stage are lit, setting the mood for tonight's play: a comedy or tragedy in one divine act. Your charmatis personae are waiting eagerly in the wings, in their bowls, tins, or bags, charging and preparing to burst onto the stage and fulfill their memorable role in this command performance.

Consider that your charms are an ensemble of actors and characters. Each piece has its own personality, voice, talent, history, and experience. Each piece also has limitations: there are things that it's not and things it can't do. This unique blend of physical and energetic attributes allows them to perform their perfect role in your casting.

You're the Director. When bonding with a potential new member of your casting ensemble, allow it to perform for you. Through this exercise, you will not only discover a core meaning for your charm, but you'll also establish many additional facets that often reveal themselves when in combination with other charms or a life area. Whenever a charm's meaning is elusive, go back to this simple dialogue, and remember, out of all of the other members of the ensemble, this charm's character, auspicious or inauspicious, has been divinely cast for a reason.

Place your charm on the stage in the image above.

Cue the Orchestra. Animate and activate a charm by letting it audition for you. Use this script as a playful guideline, and develop your own meet and greet techniques for connecting with its core characteristics. Remember to make notes in your casting grimoire as this information will prove invaluable.

Charm, hit your mark, please . . .
Now introduce yourself.

Hello!

I'm a: racing car.

I have these traits: fast, showy, competitive, elite, high-maintenance, revved up, pushing boundaries.

I am not: plodding, ordinary, user-friendly, patient, hanging around for long.

I inspire you (the caster) to feel, think or envision: expertise, admiration, envy, awe, fear, confidence, ego, adrenaline, speed, the finish line, perfection, the win, derring-do.

Pick a random charm from your kit, place it on the stage, and turn on the spotlight. Record the results of the audition.

I'm a: ______________________________

I have these traits: ______________________________

I am not: ______________________________

I inspire you to feel, think or envision: ______________________________

Think of a friend, relative, or actor or character, either fictional or living and breathing, that reminds you of this charm. What specific quality does this bring up and why?

Or

Is there an event or experience you can associate with this charm? How or where does this inhabit you in this present moment?

When a Charm "Is Not," How Is This Helpful?

Let's examine a small group of charms: The second significator, or *partner* charm, has landed in the life area of love, relationships, and emotion. There is a metal **cloud** (bad mood, confusion, or delusion) over his head which touches a **thimble** (manual and time-consuming work) also above his head. The thimble has landed inside a **ring** (marriage, commitment) and a **racing car** (speed, competition) has fallen right on top of him, pinning him down. In charmspeak, the racing car *blocks* or restrains the energy of the charm beneath it.

The cloud shows us the partner's thoughts, approach, and perspective. This reveals how he feels about having to constantly toil (thimble) on whatever's wrong with the marriage (ring). We can say that he's grumpy, moody, or confused (cloud). But what's blocking him from just doing the right thing? Let's ask the racing car!

D: Racing car, what are you?

RC: Speedy, competitive, elite . . .

D: Yes, we know all of that, but none of this resonates.

RC: (Yawns . . .)

D: OK, racing car, what are you *not*?

RC: Patient, or a fan of idling for long enough to do the time-consuming work it will take to repair the problem.

D: Thank you—and scene!

Interpretation: The partner in this reading wasn't hardwired for the thoughtful, repetitive, and detailed work on the relationship that was being expected of him. The thimble also imparts his need to protect against the prick and sting of never getting it quite right.

Compare the contrasting energies of the thimble and the racing car. The thimble is quiet, steadfast, labor-oriented, domestic; the revved-up car wants to race away from the needling (thimble), repetitive (ring) headache (clouds) of it all. Even if you find less reason to resort to this what-I'm-not technique, file it away for a rainy day at least. As you can see from the result of the racing car's audition, this piece has a lot to say. The more you're able to think outside of the charm bag, the more information you'll have at your disposal.

Before casting, try adding a few drops of your favorite magical oil, spray, or elixir to your charms and massage your hands through them, feeling them awaken, revive, and recalibrate. Once cold and inanimate, they'll become warmer to the touch. Your stage is set. Your players are in place. Listen intently as they begin to whisper, *We're ready. It's showtime!*

Good Housekeeping

Charm Lodgings: Thinking Inside and Outside of the Box

So now you have a fabulous collection of wee wild things and vagabonds. Where will they live? Happily, the hunt for the perfect home is almost as diverting as the creation of your kit. By now my eyes are trained to hone in on anything with the potential to carry my precious cargo. I received a gift. It was a miniature Bluetooth speaker and radio. Very nice. Even better, it came in a protective hard case designed to look like a suitcase. Out came the foam lining and the speaker, and in went the charms. I found a Paddington lunch tin filled with shortbread and tea. Well, let me tell you, the shortbread would make your Scottish ancestors cry, and the tea was veritable weed water. But the tin—sublime. I don't advocate the purchase of items for their containers as part of anyone's spiritual casting journey, but I thank you for being here as a support group . . .

The point is simple. Find something you love—and not just like or tolerate in the spirit of *it will make do*. Surely there's something amazing you have around your home that's temporarily storing something else. Surely that something else can temporarily find a fashionable ziplock bag. Now you're thinking! You're also imbuing your charms with another layer of your indomitable spirit and style.

Whatever storage container you decide on, just be mindful of how it closes. I know many casters like to keep their charms on their desk. But if you have to transfer your charms from *A* to *B*, then maybe just consider this: Slippery strings will open. Boxes can drop. Lids and latches will blow open. And all hell—given the slightest opportunity—is willing and able to break loose. If you decide on a box, make it a little larger so you can keep your charms in a bag inside the box.

Here are a few creative storage ideas that are both aesthetically pleasing and protective:

Vintage cigar boxes: Rustic, chic, and with hinges to allow the lid to open up and become an instant casting surface with a raised edge.

Retro lunch box: Whether the Addams Family, Edgar Allan Poe, or Curious George, you'll fall down a rabbit hole just doing an online search for your favorite theme or era. (You might even find one with a thermos.) Although roomy, again, these boxes don't have the securest latches if there's an excess of weight. Be wise, and bag your tiny treasures.

Tins and canisters: Tea, cookies, and alcohol come in the world's finest decorative and raised tins. Designed to match the decor in your home, your charms will bask in luxury. You can find these containers in a range of sizes and motifs, perfect for smaller themed kits or your rapidly expanding base kit. Note that the holiday season is prime tin time. The shop shelves are groaning under the weight of limited edition and collector tins that make casters very jolly. I'm still thanking Santa for my Jack Daniel's Old No. 7 brand—*err*—tin.

Bags: Casting from a blast from the past: that iconic, soft, purple Crown Royal bag with a gold drawstring or tarot bags and pouches. If you sew—what are you waiting for?

Artisanal, handmade, and custom-made wooden boxes and chests: Intricately hand-carved, wood-burned, finished or unfinished, and waiting for your artistic flair, these are a versatile option. DIY or support a local artist, which always feels good. You can't beat the energy and magical and fortifying properties of natural wood; it's also soft, soothing, and aromatherapeutic. Celebrate yourself. Maybe one day, consider getting one personalized.

Soapstone or stonelike composite material or resin box: Hand-carved and heavy, these sure do lend gravitas to your workspace. I once saw a rare, large hand-carved Victorian-style Incolay composite stone jewelry box. Its majesty and price tag nearly stopped my heart. And it didn't even come with sour mash. Go figure!

Glass and jars: For extra charms or smaller kits, you can find pretty relief glass boxes and cut crystal or mother-of-pearl trinket or candy jars. Some are dainty; others thick and more durable. Slightly more practical is your unassuming, down-home, wide-mouthed canning jar or a good-condition Crown or 1920s Blue Ball quart mason jar. Even if the lid is wonky, these days it's easy to search online for a specialty top, decorated with chalk, wooden, or with a lace or floral design.

Quick Aside: Antique Stores

There's nothing like walking into a shop full of century-old things, musky and musty, the quality and pride of well-crafted things, the heady sheen of a gentler generation (that pesky spirit attached to that doctor's bag). Antiquing is a relaxing way to spend an afternoon, and once you know what to look for, a caster can walk out with some inexpensive treats and treasures.

Oh, and should the proprietors puff out their chests, look down at you over spectacles perched on the bridge of their noses, and ask if they can help you, say this: *I was in the market for a Hepplewhite-splat Windsor chair circa 1780, but you don't seem to have one here, so I'll just take a look around. Bless your heart.*

Keep your eyes open for these reasonably priced items. They could very well be on a shelf right next to that Victorian chiffonier:

RCA Victor and other ancient LPs: Album covers, such as *Midnight for Two*, make fabulous kitsch casting surfaces. Want to get rid of unwanted houseguests? Just keep playing both sides of *The Three Suns with Pipe Organ.*

Beaded or sequined clutch evening bags: Perfect for a small tin of charms, a cloth, casting mala, and a few key accessories, like a mini oracle or tarot deck.

Vintage publications such as 1950s and 1960s *Life* magazines: Full of ads and illustrations, they also make fabulous casting surfaces. (see pages 173–75)

Away We Throw: Have Charms, Will Travel

If you're taking your charms on a trip, you'll want a light or stylish portable setup, a mobile home. Professional bookings notwithstanding, there's nothing better than being able to take the Wee Ones out for a ramble.

The Basic Travel Kit: Needs and Likes

Charms: base, VIP, themed or specialty kits (e.g., numbers, letters, astrology signs, word chains)

Accessories: casting surface, bowls, pointers, casting mala, pendulum, candle, matches, crystals and such, Florida water spray, tarot or oracle cards

Personal effects: hand cream, mints, lip gloss or balm, palo santo, small pad of paper, pen, grimoire, tissues, sanitizer, glasses (magnifier or a loupe) . . . to name a very few.

TRIED-AND-TRUE TIPS FOR A CHARMING GETAWAY

Checklist: Keep an inventory of your stuff in your casting grimoire. You'll be shuffling gear back and forth—from home to away then away to home. It's kinder on the nerves to rely on a list rather than an overstimulated mind, particularly if you're the throw-in-everything-but-the-kitchen-sink type.

Compression packing cubes: For a slightly larger production like an event, you'll find these double-zippered, multicolored bags handy for separating your charms, accessories, and personal effects. The mesh top panel allows you to identify the contents at a glance. When you're fresh and bright, setting up your table isn't the hardest part, unless of course, you've arrived late—*argh*—and you have a sitter that's arrived painfully early—*sigh*. It's typically at the end of a late night when you're zonked and your brain, like Elvis, has already left the building that a system helps. All you want to do is throw stuff in a bag and go home. These cubes offer generous storage and protection and stack neatly inside a carrying bag.

Travel bowls: If you have a larger base kit, your charms are probably a snug fit to the top of the tin or bag, which doesn't give you a lot of room to get your hands into the sides, corners, or bottom of the container. When you're ready to cast, you'll want to transfer your charms into a bowl. Bowls, however, are heavy and eat space. Here are some nifty travel (or home) alternatives:

Lightweight collapsible canvas dog bowls.

Valet trays. They come in different colors and sizes; They lay flat then snap together at the corners to form bowls.

Bowl cozies are the best! Roger bought a few of these from the ladies sewing circle at the Markham's District Seniors Activity Center—and I ordered more. Their superstar sewing circle makes these stunning fabric bowls in different sizes and patterns. They're designed to hold hot soup so that seniors can safely transport microwaved food to their tables. They fold and pack up like a dream. Keep your eyes open at local craft shows—and support your seniors.

If weight isn't a factor, these stylish options will have everyone complimenting your flair:

Bento boxes or colorful tin multitiered food tiffins: The top stackable container holds a small to medium set of charms; the middle one, a cloth, casting mala, miniature pointer; and the bottom—whatever else fits.

Portable and adorable organizers such as rattan suitcases: retro pinks and blues make a refreshing departure from the ol' sun, stars, and moon motif.

Vanity organizers such as train makeup cases have all the style, space, and compartments needed to take your throw on the road.

Fishing equipment tackle or craft boxes and bags: It's not the way mystics typically accessorize, but as a temporary organizer, these are waterproof, durable, and utilitarian. The more storage compartments, the merrier. Some have cantilevered trays that are great for quick identification. And nobody will suspect you'll be casting anything but lures.

Between Readings: Upkeep and Magical Spa Days

Before every casting, I wash my hands with a favorite bar of soap. It has to be a bar. It's hardly breaking news, but any personal ritual that's grounding, makes you feel good (and keeps the charms clean), and raises your vibration will enhance your connection. It's one small act of *readying.*

I also mist my charms with Florida water or add a few drops of an all-natural and aromatic product such as Madame Phoenix's Kananga Water to them. I gently massage it through the collection while asking, *Are we good? Are we ready to go?* Most of the time, they're vibrating excellently well, and we get clearance from the Spirit tower for takeoff. However, sometimes they'll feel *off,* sluggish, unresponsive—even grimy. Overworked and undersprayed!

There are two main reasons why your set might be lagging: you and others. If, as a practice, you're not balanced or grounded when divining, you can transfer this energy to your kit. If your last reading was particularly heavy or you've been doing a lot of back-to-back readings for both yourself and sitters, you might need more than a few invigorating drops of cologne. If your charms have been sitting idle for a while, they can also go into what I call energetic hibernation and feel stale. Regardless, when your sacred tool stops whispering and begins grumbling—and you will know when that happens—it's time to reattune and treat them to a spa day.

There's no right or wrong way to energetically cleanse and glow-up your charms. Rely on your own personal beliefs and practices, because it's the intention behind the act that will matter. Some casters work well with smoke—wafts of palo santo, sage, sacred tobacco, or resins. Others work with high-vibrating crystals or treat their kit to an overnight staycation in the light of a full moon. I prefer warm water and a bar of charcoal soap.

Light your favorite candle. Set the mood with some atmospheric music. Begin by removing any charms that could potentially be damaged by the water and handle them separately. Fill up a bowl or your bathroom sink with a few inches of hot water, and prepare a towel. Get a good lather on your soap and dip it into the bath. Now, carefully, give your charms a soothing soak. Rub them between your fingers, then bring them back out for a good and (very) thorough towel dry. You may even notice some tiny chips and sludge at the bottom of the bowl—detritus that's broken or rubbed off your pieces. You'll just love the way they look and feel once they're back in their tin, all frisky, bright-eyed and bushy-tailed.

Tip: It's very rare, but this can happen. You find or receive a piece, and it's dark, not only with surface dirt but a questionable energetic imprint. If this occurs, give it a good sound bath. Place it in a Tibetan singing bowl. Strike the bowl on the outside with a mallet; lightly drag the mallet along the lip; and let that long, resonant frequency clear away the gunk.

Scribble

Wondering about the energetic state of your set? Ask your charms. Randomly select a piece before and then after cleansing. Who did they elect as their spokescharms? What was the message? How cool would it be, if the same charms reappeared the next time, too.

Charmventory

If you can, it's advisable to keep a master list of your charms so that you can do a complete inventory. Unlike a fixed deck of thirty-six, fifty-two, or seventy-eight cards that, for the most part, behave and are easily spotted once airborne, charms are ninjas and stealth artists—and oops, there goes another one—*how many did I have?* It's a drag reading without a major player. It's also a laugh riot when three of the five landed charms carry the same core meaning—or are exactly the same. Weirder things have happened. Mostly, if, over time, you've decided to combine a few kits.

A charmventory is not only a roll call for your pieces, but an opportunity to get a big-picture and hands-on analysis of your ensemble: the balance, aesthetics, quality, vitality, efficiency, organization, and magnitude. You'll identify pieces that are either damaged, or no longer speak or stand up for you, and you'll revisit the oddballs: the I-♥-this frog in a cowboy hat, but *what did it mean again?* Charmventories are definitely rainy-day projects, but so advantageous: this is how a collection of random trinkets and trifles flourish into a forever kit.

Taking It to the Table

You're going to lay out each piece on a table. Here's the key thing: If you have a medium to large collection, you'll want to get through this time-consuming stage as quickly as possible so you can begin the actual charmventory. Organize your charms into groups according to *what* they are and not their meanings. It takes two seconds to identify a *rocking horse* as a piece of *furniture,* and much longer to contemplate its role. That comes next.

Here are some examples of groupings:

Hearts and keys; rings; flowers and plants; tools, professional trades (adding or sewing machine, spool) and implements (shovel, spade, hammer); health, wellness, and health care; weapons and nasty, sharp things (axe, hook, arrowhead); buildings; connectors, pointers and bars; chains and bracelets; animals, reptiles, insects, and birds (whether real, character, or mythical such as rubber ducky or phoenix); archaeological (dinosaur); sports and leisure; home: furniture, appliances, decor; coins, tokens, dice, and money; gemstones; beads and seeds; sea life and shells; body parts; people; human characters; transportation (jeep, plane, parachute); weather (lightning bolt, clouds); seasons and elements; clothing and accessories (purse, crown, headphones); career (fire department symbol); electronic, technology; spirituality, faith, death, and afterlife (ghosts, skulls); fasteners, pins, and buttons; food, drink, and smokes (pipe); planets, luminaries, and zodiac (stars, moons, suns); education; landscape, earth, geography, and navigation (mountains, globe, compass rose); time; music, theater, and art; game pieces (dominoes, tiles, and pawns); shapes and spirals.

If you're spending more than two seconds on categorizing a charm, push it temporarily into a miscellaneous pile and come back to it at the end.

Phew, That's Over. Now What?

You have your last piece in place and you're staring out at an impressive charmscape. Now start with one group. Pull all of the pieces in front of you and go through them one by one. Address them by their meanings. You might have duplicates that are variations on a theme, **subcategory or descriptor** charms that give you a more nuanced interpretation. That's OK. Weed out the obvious (exact same charm) or unnecessary and unwanted duplicates (similar meaning).

Charmventories allow you to recall why you have three snakes. One is ready to strike; the other is slithering low in the grass; the third is made of jade and heralds a financial threat or complication. Great. They can all stay. Why do you have four chairs? One's a director's chair—*control and calling the shots*—another is a wheelchair—*health or mobility issues.* Next is a reclining beach chair—*relaxation or vacation.* And then there's the throne—*empowerment and sovereignty.* But wait a minute, you also have a crown that means the same as the throne. Now you have a decision to make. Will you keep the throne and alter the meaning—*a psychic medium's chair*, perhaps? Or put it in a keepsake jar for a future themed kit?

Pull out a few kindred pieces that belong to the same group and play. For instance, furniture and our four chairs. Challenge these charms by casting them in a hypothetically unusual role. Imagine that your sitter's asked the question: *What will X be like in a committed relationship*? Mix your charms up in front of you and pull one. Lounge chair? What do you think? *Will this new person be easy? Relaxed? Or bone idle?* What would the other pieces say?

And one more thing: look at your hands. Are they filthy? You know what to do next. That's right: book a spa day.

> *The world is full of magic things,*
> *patiently waiting for our senses to grow sharper.*
> —W. B. Yeats

Reading Surfaces

MUST-HAVE AND MAKE ACCESSORIES

The Pointer: The Charm Caster's Magic Wand

Every time I do a large casting, without exception, I look at the charmscape—this fantastic confusion of items, like a charm bracelet's just been fired out of a cannon—and think, *WTF?! What now? I can't feel my head.* What reasonable explanation is there for this depth of dread? Dementors, surely. Then I reach for my pointer. Somehow, just holding and aiming a stick at seemingly impossible work is reassuring and stabilizing. It can make you feel smarter, more composed, and less likely to implode. It will allow you to concentrate and direct your focus and purpose into the pointer. *Expecto Patronum*: it's the charm caster's magic wand.

A few tips—*err*—pointers: Without question, a good pointer will become your must-have, go-to, can't-live-without accessory. What does it do? Trick question: It points. It also lifts—and separates. By letting the tip hover over a specific charm or a small section, it breaks the casting down into bite or brain-sized pieces so you don't take in too much at once.

Look for a pointer ideally six to ten inches long that has a sharp, narrow, and tapered tip. If you can, try and keep your fingers out of your casting. Once you've thrown your pieces, they've stepped into their roles, and it's like you're tramping through their performance, physically and energetically. I can hear them screaming: *Get off the stage!* Understandably, there will be times when you may have to overturn a reversed 2D charm to see what it is or examine a clump. If and whenever you can, use your pointer to gently shift or move a piece to see what lies beneath. It's cleaner, more respectful, and it stops you from messing up the presentation because those exact details—the longitude, latitude, architecture, charmscape—can all carry layers of subtle but useful information.

Traditional and nontraditional pointers: African porcupine quills (beautiful—and very sharp), vintage knitting needles, funky cocktail stirrers, mini wands. I just recently found battery-operated LED chopsticks that glow in both red and purple light. In my travel kit, I also have a few mini (3.5 inches) glittery plastic cuticle pushers. Don't judge.

Going to the Mat

There's a thriving online market for anyone looking to purchase a stylized, graphically designed casting mat with a rubbery or velvety surface. In my experience, there's one potential drawback with a commercial casting mat: you're always locked into an artistic or divinatory framework that isn't your own.

These mats are available in a range of shapes, sizes, colors, and aesthetics. Often they're square but feature a circle divided into segments dedicated to the various life areas: money, love and relationships, health and spirituality, for example. In the beginning, this is a no-brainer. It's a good way to ease into charm casting with training wheels because the broad strokes are all laid out for you. The design elements can include prompt words, letters, numbers, and images or clip-arty symbols to assist you and simplify the process of interpretation. And should this be your personal preference, then by all means, fair winds and following seas. Stick with it.

Ponder the following before investing in a casting mat.

Is It the Right Size?

Temper the mat's visual allure with a rational assessment of your workspace, habits, and technique. How much of your criteria does it meet? Take some time to consider whether or not it's the right fit for your work area. Is it portable (if that matters)? How's your throwing arm? If you're a *sprinkler*—a few charms here and there—will you need to book an Uber to get from one charm to another? Conversely, if you like to sauce and toss the lot, you'll need extra real estate. While clumps are an integral part of a casting, who wants their charms piling into a rugby scrum? No one. That's who.

Does the Mat Resonate with You as a Spiritual Tool?

Or is it a just an engaging piece of artwork featuring phrasing, images, placement, or proportioning that are more addling than useful? Let me explain. If a mat's too busy, it can be perceived as *noisy*. Too many unnecessary or anomalous design elements can argue with or slow down the intuitive process. They can create a chi-exhausting layer of dissonance and distraction, like something running invisibly in the background of your hard drive. It's possible to react subconsciously to any of these kinds of things:

- One image or area that's markedly larger than another
- Words that you wish were or weren't there or phrased differently to suit your charmspeak
- An imbalance between auspicious and inauspicious symbols or their placement
- Letters or numbers taking up prime real estate. It's not a Ouija board, and you might not even want them there for every reading.
- Too many superfluous elements, dots, lines, flourishes. Why?
- Novelty themes, the novelty of which could wear out

- Four corner design elements that adequately fill white space, but feel unhelpful
- You like most of it, but be it conscious or unconscious, there's just something that's . . . not . . . quite . . . tickety-boo, but you settle anyway because what are your alternatives?

Take some time to study a potential surface. See how you feel, because unconsciously, these seemingly small factors can also bias your reading. If you're only using a few pieces (three to ten charms), this may not be as big of an issue; however, in a larger casting, you're going to want to be able to soft gaze and scry the charmscape—the landscape of the casting. You'll need enough bandwidth to focus purely on the intricacies of patterns, shapes, lines, themes, directionality, energy, voice, and the many facets of meaning available for each individual oracle. Quite simply put, it's like the difference between how you feel in the country as opposed to a bustling city. Simplicity and a soothing sightline promote an ability to hear yourself think. Horns, sirens, and traffic aren't conducive to the diviner becoming the clearest and calmest channel for Spirit. And give a thought to your tiny treasures. Will they have to shout over the commotion just to be heard?

Q: I don't decoupage or have the skills or central nervous system for graphic design. Is there still a way that I can personalize my reading surface and streamline my method?

A: I'm glad you asked. Yes, there most definitely is. And it all begins with these next few DIY projects. But before we can segue into these alternatives, let's address an all-too-common charm casting challenge.

UFOs: Unauthorized Flying Objects

Tiny and lightweight, the trinkets and trifles we casters work with can be tricky. Why? How do we say this politely? We don't.

Frankly, they may be cute, but they're also lively little buggers that like to bounce all over hell's half acre. The more intricate the design on your floor, the more they want to play hide-and-seek. This isn't an endearing quality because the Roomba is the natural predator of the casting charm. Also their desire to take up residence behind or underneath furniture or an appliance is indirectly proportionate to the ease of retrieving them from these hard-to-reach places. You might not even know they've flown the coop. They're shifty like that. For the record, we call these unauthorized flying objects *jumpers*.

Textured mats can help calm down a leap or dampen a roll, but that's all. Fortunately, there are a few things you can do to keep your baubles from bolting.

Trays, Lids, and Boxes

A sure method of controlling jumpers is to fortress the reading. One way of doing this is to choose a surface with built-in walls or raised sides and lips that essentially create a baby gate. Wooden boxes or metal tins can offer a dual function. They not only act as a storage container, but can also come with a removable or hinged lid to serve as a surface.

You may want to fit or more permanently attach some fabric or leather into this surface. For one thing, it looks good. But it also absorbs the impact of the landing, which bodes well for the longevity of your more fragile pieces.

You can find wooden, no-frills cafeteria or more decorative trays that help detain UFOs. They're also perfect for impromptu couch or lap readings. And then there's this advantage: if you need to transport a divination from one room to another without disturbing the architecture of the reading, yeah, trays are just the thing.

> *Nature is pleased with simplicity.*
> *And nature is no dummy.*
> —Isaac Newton

The Joy of the Plain: Vintage, Antique, Lace, Linen, and Cotton Cloths

Both inspiring and intimidating in equal parts, there's nothing like a blank canvas that celebrates you the artist and your charms, the color palette. There are no paint-by numbers, no visual prompts or superfluities. Just a clean, unassuming backdrop that highlights instead of pulling focus from your charms. Like soft white sand peppered with seashells, plain cloth is quiet, neutral, and expansive, calming for both eyes and spirit: this is where mastery begins.

Take a look around your home for any plain, single-color linens, cloth napkins, or handkerchiefs. My 97-year-young aunt had a cupboard full, all fastidiously starched and folded. Alternatively, add this to a must-find list for your next thrift or antique store outing. You can definitely uncover some beautiful and inexpensive 12-by-12 handkerchiefs with straight or lacey, scalloped edges. Throw a casting mala around it and you're ready to work. This size is small enough for a daily or quick-pull casting, but can also handle a deeper dive of two pudgy fingerfuls. If you have the sprawling workspace and want more pieces, by all means, find that fabric or piece of leather that best accommodates the style and scope of your casting. Added, of course, to the many advantages of plain-surface casting is that cloths are portable and often fit perfectly into the same tin or bag as your charms.

Just like when you go hunting and gathering for charms and their lodgings, be as creative as you like when looking for your cloth. Who knew that I'd be casting on a 20-by-25 soft, woven cotton hand towel by lantern light with charms gleaming in an antique enamel bowl (husband asking, *Why are you dressed like Martha Washington?*)?

Grandma's Way

Starching and Ironing Your Casting Cloths

For a fresh, crisp cloth with all the romantic vibes of a bygone era, starch and iron your casting surface. This works a charm on light-colored and natural fabrics like cotton or linen.

In a **large measuring cup**, add 1 tablespoon full of cornstarch to 2 cups cold water.

Stir well with a **wooden spoon** until dissolved. It will turn milky.

Add a few drops of your favorite **essential oil**. Heavenly.

Using a **funnel**, pour the solution into a **spray bottle**. It won't last forever as the cornstarch will eventually settle into a sludge at the bottom of your spray bottle, so **label** it in **marker** with a date to remind yourself to shake before next use. Place in a dark, cold place—like a fridge.

Lightly spray your cloth. Let the starch settle into the fibers. Wait a bit. Then iron.

Know your iron. Read your guidelines for the correct heat settings. You can also use a hot pan.

If this becomes your new favorite thing to do, you may have to eventually clean your iron's faceplate. Use white vinegar on a cloth.

If you really want those romantic Victorian and cottagecore vibes, hang the cloth on a line in the sun. (Then press it to your face because it smells like childhood.)

If you keep this cloth folded, when you open it, the lines instantly divide your surface into four quarters.

Meet the Charmala: A Versatile Reading System Built into a DIY Accessory

Before this breakthrough, there was buffoonery: years of crawling around the floor looking for jumpers, searching for flashlights (then batteries), and what else—*argh*—sifting through vacuum cleaner dust cups. That happened. Then, mercifully, an epiphany. Hardly original, it was, however, a game-changer. I was heading out and rushing through those finishing touches in the mirror. Blinking furiously, trying to air-dry some mascara, I grabbed a glittery, black string of (imitation) Austrian crystal beads. Well, it almost made it over my head. Instead, I bolted to my desk and formed a circle thinking, *AHA! Party's over, you runaways and fugitives. Meet your new fence.*

This was my first casting mala, necessity clearly being the mother of invention. My surface area now had structure and definition; the necklace acted like a barricade for the disobedient. Soon after, it blew up into its own thing. What initially began as a relaxing project, eventually resulted in an infinitely more fun and fine divining experience.

Here again, I'd like to pay homage to traditional bone readers who throw into a circle divided into quadrants known as the crossroads. They designate meaning to each quadrant and interpret the pieces according to how they've landed in these areas. By no means is the following casting mala system a reinvention of the sacred wheel; it's just a reimagining with the kitsch caster's spin. But, given time, love, and patience, it can turn your charm casting method on its head.

The Circle of Life: Reading with a Charmala

No doubt, you're familiar with the sacred japamala or mala. It's a circuit of 108 prayer beads separated by tiny knots. Typically, it also features an extra, distinctive guru or buddha bead and a tassel or some other focal piece, like a quartz crystal. Well, now you're going to learn all about the *charmala*, or the *jumpmala.*

This DIY loop of beads will serve two key functions:

Discourage the more high-spirited Wee Ones from going AWOL. (Because, as we've already discussed, nobody needs the extra hassle of having to remove the heating vent or cat to see where the eagle landed.)

and

Become a deeply personal, portable, multicontext alternative to an illustrated casting mat. You'll have a handy structure of four quadrants, twelve houses, and numerology lines or paths, as well as a clock dial that, if this intention is set, helps you divine the timing of an experience or event. First, you'll learn how to bead in your compass points, and then we'll dive into the many ways of applying it.

The Twelve-Point Charmala Rose

There won't be a pop quiz, I promise. Still, getting a rudimentary understanding of this concept in advance will help you divine the lay of the land moving forward. You'll soon begin viewing your casting mala with the trained eye of an explorer: the possibilities, directions, and potential are literally uncharted. And it has this advantage: As the context for any reading changes, you're free to reimagine your wheel accordingly and activate a brand-new set of intentions.

Imagine a simple eight-point compass rose, also called a star or wind rose. It appeared on mariner's charts to show the orientation of the four cardinal directions (true north, east, south, and west) and the four intercardinal directions (NE, SE, SW, NW): the eight principal winds that billowed through their sails.

As casters, we're also going to take a 360-degree beaded circle and divide it into four equal areas. Then further divide each of these quadrants into thirds, which will give us a total of twelve segments and twelve invisible borders. The goal here is to mindfully create a reading structure that's informed by the perimeter of your casting surface.

To breeze through the beading process, let's agree on a few terms. Let's call the four main sections *quarters*; the twelve segments *houses*; and the twelve borders *lines* or *paths*. By using slightly different and bigger beads, you'll be marking

four *cardinal* points (T, top; B, bottom; L, left; R, right) and eight *intercardinal* points. After you've set intentions, assigning meaning to each of these points, quarters, houses, and boundary lines, just like that your twelve-point charmala rose becomes an indispensable navigational tool.

How Will This Work?

Connect the opposing dots between the four cardinal points, and you'll have an equal-armed cross that defines the four quarters or crossroads. Like any wheel, your twelve houses and paths are arranged radially, like spokes. After setting your intentions, you'll come to rely on these points to provide the coordinates of charms when they land. When casting into your charmala, these lines will be visible to your mind's eye, and if you ever have any doubt, all you have to do is hover your pointer over the charmala rose and instantly get your bearings. With a bit of practice, you'll soon be anchored in your own divinatory method and vision.

Let's bead on, shall we?

Creating a Casting Mala

Three Charmalas: In a Nutshell

The Jumpmala: Find any old necklace with more or less but *ideally* the same size and color 6–10 mm beads. Simply lay it around any reading surface. Keep calm and cast on.

The Charmala Rose: Create and bead your own beautifully nuanced casting mala from scratch. Glittery, glowing, wooden, metal, or energetic gemstone—choose beads that reflect your preferences, personality, and magical practice. Be the master of your own divination ceremonies. This has a built-in reading system that can be used for any context. It features four cardinal and eight (different) intercardinal impact beads that help form four quadrants, twelve houses or life areas, a clock dial, and numerological lines.

The Circle of Life Charmala: This is a variation of the charmala rose featuring perimeter charms attached via jump rings at twelve equidistant points, either in lieu of the impact beads, or at midpoint, in between these cardinal and intercardinal beads to label the houses. Why do this? It gives you all of the same built-in mapping, but will be superhelpful if you're committed to a certain method of reading that favors a *fixed* set of symbols. The zodiac wheel is a great example. The charms sitting on the outside of your casting surface not only mark the location of the houses, but now impart their astrological meaning to these segments. Or you can employ a general circle of life, where selected charms represent your main life areas or hot topics.

> This charmala best mimics a pie-shaped casting map, but you'll be throwing onto a cleaner casting surface and have more control over the framework.

How many charmalas do you need? All you need is one. That said, I've made a few, including a multipurpose general charmala, one for relationship castings, and a special Girls' Night Out charmala. They all perform the same way and can be used interchangeably; it's the choice of beads, color, composition, and intention that imparts the palpable difference in their personalities and energies. My relationship charmala glints with Austrian crystal hearts—and the romance and sparkle of tiny, shiny spacers flanked by red roses. The Girls' Night Out charmala is a circle of life featuring twelve plump, colorful 3D perimeter charms and glowing beads. It's client-friendly and often an icebreaker. The resin pale peach and purple stemmed cocktail, luminous seashell, and pudgy pink teddy bear keep my sitters bemused, happy, and chill. This is a welcome alternative to the predictable question of "You're not going to tell me something bad or scary, right?" (Define *bad* or *scary*?)

You might worry: *Surely, this downplays the sanctity and seriousness of divination.* I can safely say that after you've done many readings and received validation of accuracy and value, you'll become sympatico with your process—whatever that looks like. How you window-dress your "table" has nothing to do with becoming the clearest and most accurate channel for messages. It's all about delivering divine guidance that can provide clarity and actionable steps. Messages should always be channeled through a filter of compassion—and sometimes, a bright pink flamingo. It can't hurt!

You Will Need

A quick FYI: This is a list of the supplies and gear that I've been using. By all means, explore the wealth of YouTube videos on the subject and trust your own talent. I'm not an expert at beading, crafting, or jewelry making.

Yet, surprisingly, my own charmalas have stood the test of time. Once done, you'll sit back and be amazed by the powerful magic that you've imparted to your tool.

- ☐ 6 and/or 8 mm beads, max. 164
- ☐ 4–24 of these beads should be different (in size or color) than the other 140 (I'll explain in a bit.)
- ☐ Spacers (optional)
- ☐ Findings and jewelry tools. They often come together in a kit. Get a small kit with different-sized open (or split) jump rings. Also, if you're going to attach charms to your casting mala, you'll need 12 extra perimeter charms with a bail or loop—that aren't from your kit.
- ☐ Beading board (optional yet highly recommended). The grooves not only keep the beads from running feral, but also help you see and design your pattern before the beading begins.
- ☐ 0.8 mm stretchy elastic cord for making jewelry (I love this because your cut end is thick enough to use as a beading needle. It also knots well and is durable.)
- ☐ If you have real mala skills and are adept at making those tiny knots, you might prefer using a cotton, linen, or hemp cord.
- ☐ A tube of Krazy or E6000 jewelry glue (optional)
- ☐ A bit of string to mark a place
- ☐ Scissors
- ☐ Any bracelet that keeps its shape (If you're not keen on making a matching one with leftover beads.)

Murphy's Law and the Charmala SNAFU

What's Murphy's law? Who's Murphy anyway? And, more importantly, what's this got to do with my charmala?

As we all know, toast always lands jam and buttery side down. Whatever can go wrong—will go wrong. And that's Murphy's law.

Edward Aloysius Murphy Jr. was an American aerospace engineer and former (not to mention really handsome) World War II pilot. In the late 1940s, he was called in to help the U.S. Air Force with a very Top Gun project. To make a long story short, there was a SNAFU, and it malfunctioned. Colorful words followed. Over time, they were distilled into an adage now known as Murphy's law. It reminds us of the benefit of having a good defensive strategy and the importance of *anticipation* to avoid the aggravation of a situation normal: all fouled up—SNAFU.

What charm(s) might you use to represent anticipation, Murphy's law, or a SNAFU? ____________________________________

____

How to Make the Charmala Rose

Start by deciding how large you want your wheel to be. My charmalas range from 10 to 14 inches in diameter. They all feature the same twelve-point compass rose, but vary in the number, sizes, and types of beads in each quarter.

When selecting beads for your cardinal and intercardinal points, keep in mind that these twelve points will act as fence posts and orientation guides, providing an instant, at-a-glance reference. This is how you begin beading in a reading *system*. When casting on a plain, unillustrated surface, you'll come to rely on these impact beads to define boundaries, show you your lines, and tell you where the quadrants and houses begin and end, as well as any numbered lines. Depending on what intentions you've set, they'll signify hours on a clock dial, months, numbers, seasons, zodiac signs, life areas, special topics, house meanings—and so much more. So you'll want these to stand out. Think of these twelve beads—the four cardinals and eight intercardinals—as your queen beads; and the others, the ones that compromise the main body of your string, as the worker beads.

Designing Your Pattern

Your all-star lineup of beads and spacers is called a pattern. Before you start committing your beads to the cord, take some time to design your pattern, ideally using a grooved beading board, which keeps the beads corralled as you lay your work out in front of you, make tweaks, and settle on a bead count. If numerology factors into your practice, consider using a meaningful count of seven, nine, or eleven beads for each section between your twelve points. (Tiny spacer beads aren't counted.)

Decide, in advance, if you'd prefer a simple string or a variegated pattern that could also include decorative 3–4 mm spacers separating each bead. Again, there are some brilliant YouTube mala mentors online who will patiently walk you through the art of tying knots between beads, if that's more to your liking.

A Handy Checklist for the Charmala Rose

- ☐ 4 cardinal (or impact) beads that are different from the intercardinals
- ☐ 8 smaller (or spacer) beads to flank your cardinal bead

- ☐ 8 intercardinal beads (uniquely colored or shaped—you want these to be smaller than your cardinals, but still larger or different from the rest)
- ☐ 16 spacer beads to flank the intercardinal beads

It's up to you how many 6–8 mm beads you want between your points. Consider using four different colors for each quarter. For example, if you decide that each quarter represents a season or an element, use the same-colored beads for that one section to differentiate it from the other three.

Your spacers can all be varied; they are, after all, the spice of the wheel of life.

A sample seven-count beading pattern

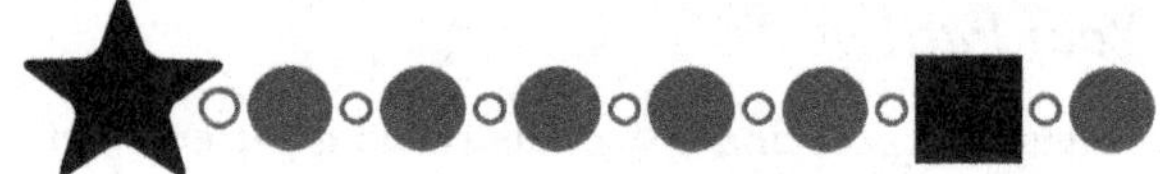

First cardinal bead (12 mm)—(6 mm spacer)—8 mm bead—(3 mm spacer)—8 mm bead—(3 mm spacer)—8 mm bead—(3 mm spacer)—8 mm bead—(3 mm spacer)—8 mm bead—(3 mm spacer)—first intercardinal bead (10 mm)—(3 mm spacer)—8 mm bead . . .

Stretchy Cord and Murphy

What's the worst thing that can happen? Well, for instance you've masterfully strung three-quarters of your charmala, and one of the cut ends of elastic cord snakes off your board or table. What now? You're right if you guessed a trip to the swear jar. Beads and spacers are flung everywhere like a hailstorm. It's a few hours of your life you'll never get back.

So what did we learn from the handsome young Murphy? Anticipation. Whatever can go wrong will go wrong, so be smart on the front end. Experienced beaders cut both ends of a length of cord and tie a knot on the opposite side. You can also just leave the spool on the table and work with one cut end as your beading needle. Keep pulling extra cord as needed, ensuring that you have a good length of cord on your working end, then cut the other right before you knot the two ends together. This has worked well for me, and so far, the swear jar is only half full.

How to Make the Circle of Life Charmala

In terms of beading, there's one important difference with a circle of life. The more basic charmala rose features twelve impact beads. But, if you're attaching perimeter charms in lieu of your impact beads, your jump rings will need to sit between two beads at these points, so when creating your pattern, choose twelve *pairs* of beads for these locations.

Start beading with only one of your top pair of cardinal beads; then finish the circle by adding the other partner bead. You're doing this because you'll be tying the knot in the center of these two beads. This helps you tuck and hide the knotted cord within the jump ring.

Once the mala's finished and your knot tied and glued, attach your twelve perimeter charms. Account for any differences in size and width for these perimeter charms before you begin attaching them. Obviously, a plump strawberry won't sit the same way as a flatter charm. For bigger charms, you can use two jump rings. This will allow them to sit out a bit farther so it doesn't raise the charmala awkwardly at these points.

Tying the Knot

Make a simple knot, passing the left cord over the right cord then underneath twice. Now, pass the right cord over the left, and bring it around twice. Pull taut. This should do it, but reverse and repeat if necessary.

Giving your cord a gentle stretch before stringing any beads helps stop your charmala from stretching out further once beaded.

Tighten your knot from on the top and bottom; gently pull and tighten both the top loose ends and the bottom beaded sides of the cord.

Optionally, after cutting your ends, add a dab of glue into the heart of your knot. E6000 jewelry glue is the popular choice.

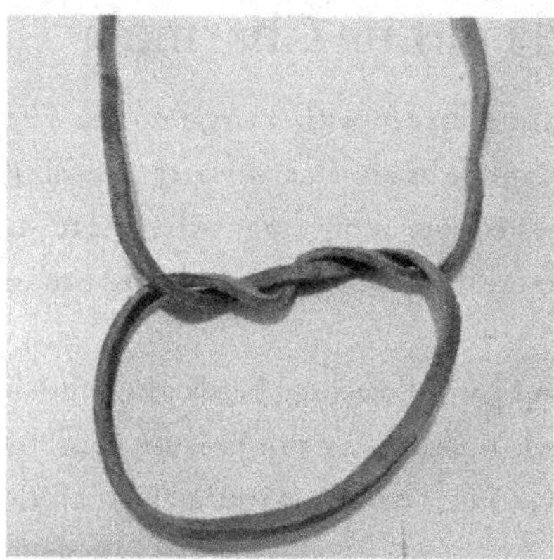

The Anatomy of a Charmala

TIMING, NUMEROLOGY, AND CASTROLOGY

The Seer's Bull's-Eye

If you're not using a casting mat with an illustrated center, you'll need a small bracelet to place in the middle of your circle. We'll call this the seer's bull's-eye. Charms that land in this area will speak to the core, heart, or theme of the reading or demand your full attention in the present. You can always just use one of your bracelets or bangles. Better yet, why not use your leftover worker beads to create a dazzling centerpiece that matches your charmala. It won't require any queen beads and takes hardly any extra time.

And so, the wheel begins to turn.
Charms, where y'at?

It's just you now, with a tin, bowl, or bag of tiny treasures and your beautiful charmala circling a plain, unillustrated cloth. You sprinkle a few charms into and around the casting surface. Without the structure and certainty of design elements, there are moments when you'll sit scratching your head, wondering, *Charms, where y'at?* Until, of course, you've energized the areas both inside and outside of your casting surface.

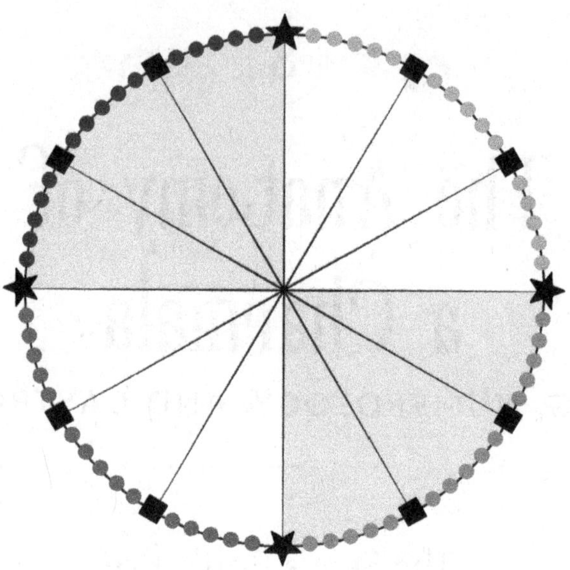

Anatomy of the Charmala: Let's Review and Contemplate.

Your pieces can only land in a few places:

Inside, touching, or sitting on the edge of the **seer's bull's-eye** in the center of your circle.

Out of play. Somewhere on the other side of the *fence* or charmala.

In a **quadrant of the main circle**: top left, top right, bottom left, or bottom right: Designate these areas any way that you want. You can keep these quarters the same or set new intentions every casting.

On or around a line extending from an impact bead to the center: Each line represents a **numbered path**, 1–12, and carries its own meaning. You can apply the meanings in the section below or rely on your own knowledge of numerology.

In the **houses**, the twelve segments of your circle. Assign your own general life area meaning to each sector, or anchor your reading in astrology, applying the characteristics of the six personal and six impersonal houses of the zodiac.

Tip: If, like me, you don't have an eidetic memory, keep cue cards in a plastic pocket of your casting grimoire with the twelve house and numerological path meanings.

In the Name of the Rose: Charging the Charmala

How will you best use your charmala's quadrants, houses, lines, seer's bull's-eye, and surrounding area?

You've created a casting mala, infused it with your own energy, given it a spark and personality, but now it's time to give it purpose. The charmala rose is a multipurpose tool. Its impact beads are generic, so they can be assigned any task or meaning. In essence, they act as sentinels, vigilantly awaiting instruction. Before any casting, you'll have to decide on an approach. What kind of reading are you doing? Will you only be working with the assigned meanings for the four quadrants? Are you asking about timing? Will you use all or just a part of the available framework? Once you've settled on a system, your charms can land anywhere on a plain, unillustrated surface, and the synthesis between the what and the where will merge blissfully into clear and unmistakable messages. Trust that once your beads are strung and your intentions communicated, this rose will begin to bloom.

Addressing the Four Quarters

How will you charge your circle's quarters?

For the moment, forget about all of the potential layers of meaning of houses and numbered paths. Let's set an intention to cast solely using the four quarter meanings and seer's bull's-eye.

Lay your charmala down on a plain cloth; form a circle. Lay your bracelet down in the middle. Envision an equal-armed cross in the middle that separates four quadrants. Now make it sacred: name and claim your personal quarters.

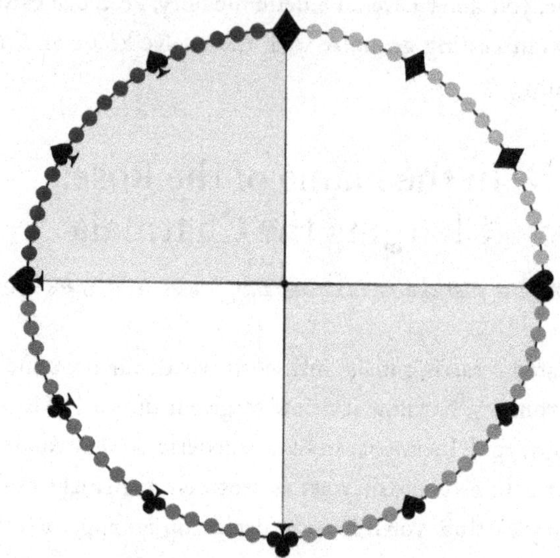

Quarter Notes: The Elements, Tarot, or Playing Card Suits

Cartomancers, like philosophers, passionately subscribe to different schools of thought about the correspondences for the four suits found in both playing cards and the tarot. Just pick and stick with your favorite. And while we're on that topic, quick question: Does the element of earth belong in the top left quadrant? Or is that water? There's no right or wrong way—just your way. You do you! Develop your own system and style. These are just a few suggestions to get you started.

Earth (pentacles, clubs, autumn): passive, the tangible, mundane, and monetary; service, work, steadfast and sure-footed progress, reliability, groundedness, dedication, and effort; the body. Autumn is associated with winding down, harvest and bounty based on spring's efforts. *Shadow:* greed, materialism, inflexibility, stubbornness, resentful of spirit; unevolved, plodding.

Water (cups, hearts, summer): passive, love, emotion, creativity, flow; family, sun-kissed, fulfilled wishes and desires, all good, empathic, receptive. Summer is associated with growing, ripening, flourishing, thriving. *Shadow:* moody, self- or overindulgent, idealistic.

Fire (wands, diamonds, spring): active, will, the big yes, ambition, action; spirit, dynamism, magnetism; psychic abilities. Spring is associated with new beginnings, planting, nurturing, tending, effort, and perseverance. *Shadow:* egotistical, vainglorious, overbearing, scorching, defiant, unstable and unpredictable, manipulative.

Air (swords, spades, winter): active, intellect, wit, hardships and lessons, the big no, the diametric opposite of hearts, wishes and desires unfulfilled, loss, challenges, sorrows, lessons, transition and downturns. Winter is associated with resting, resisting, disconnecting, and cooling; *Ice, ice baby! Shadow:* hardship, endings, restriction, resistance, conflict, and violence.

No Quarter

If a charm falls directly on the *X* in the middle of the bracelet, might this herald a major decision and an unavoidable turning point? What feels right to you?

What if one lands directly on a quarter line? There are many ways to read charms that land on these lines. It's like they are stuck at a border awaiting inspection and clearance. You could decide that these charms take on a bit of both quarters; or read the charm anatomically. Use the example of the mushroom where the cap is in one quarter and the stem in the other, or try assigning clear meanings for each of these lines. Also, remember to check a charm's directionality. Is it pointing somewhere or at something? Is that where it wants to go but for some reason can't? Or is it trying to send something to another charm? You'll learn to trust your intuition and soft gaze about information that exists not only on but also between the lines.

YOUR PERSONAL QUARTERS

ASSIGNING PURPOSE

In your grimoire, create a dream theme for a future casting.

- Think of a theme or context for your reading, such as a daily dive, self-love, relationships, business, spiritual evolution, energy management or wellness.
- Imagine meanings for each quarter and border lines.
- Develop a few keywords to describe each quarter.

SAMPLE

Context: *Best Use of My Day.*
Center: *Key Message, what wants my attention.*

Top Left Quarter: *Expect this.*
Keywords: *How might I be predisposed to greet the day, events, or emotions?*

Bottom Left Quarter: *Embrace this.*
Keywords: *Focus on this gift, strength, resource. Seek this wisdom.*

Bottom Right Quarter: *Resist this.*
Keywords: *Contemplate or avoid this way of thinking, acting, reacting, or behaving.*

Top Right Quarter: *Manifest this.*
Keywords: *Free will decisions that create a productive or happy day*

Charmala Time: The Clock and Calendar

In the beginning, physically bond and attune with your charmala before every casting: Rub a little essential oil on your fingers. Start with the first, top cardinal bead at 12 o'clock. It helps to lightly place your finger and energy on each of the twelve impact beads and, circling clockwise, also mentally draw a path with your finger (from the bead to the center), while silently focusing on your timings. Your twelve impact beads can represent hours or months; and your quarters, weeks or seasons. Or you can work using the numbered paths as a general timeline, where anything falling around 1 o'clock happens first, before any incidents concluding at 11 or 12. Your clock is your own, and so you set the hands according to what feels right. If 12 o'clock, the very top feels like *now*, then set those intentions.

Timing might not be a concern or focus for every one of your readings. And as we all know, *divining* timing is a tricky proposition because the future is always in flux and subject to free will choices. That said, the time you invest energizing your charmala's built-in calendar and clock will pay dividends. Should you need validation on something specific, once you are attuned you'll be able to ask that your charms confirm or show you something by landing on or in these charged areas.

When Will or Did This Happen?

While most of your timing queries will start in the present and extend into the future, you can also use your charmala to isolate when, exactly, something occurred in the past or will happen in the future. Assign a date or an event to the top impact bead. It's like going into your online banking transactions and establishing a date range. Let's say that your house is going to be put on the market on a specific date in the coming months. Naturally, you're interested in divining the immediacy and timing of the first offer. When addressing your top cardinal impact bead, use the date the For Sale sign is planted on the lawn, and break the rest of the charmala down into weeks or months. Now let your charms do the rest of the work of revealing challenges, auspicious dates, and the likelihood of wishes fulfilled or unfulfilled.

Numerology: Reading the Charmala's Twelve Lines

You've beaded a versatile structure into your charmala that not only allows you to charge twelve houses, but also to weave in additional layers of meaning to twelve lines or paths. Each line or numerological path runs from your queen beads to the hive: the center or hub of your wheel. Count clockwise from 12—your top bead. The next intercardinal bead is 1; the next intercardinal bead, 2, and so on.

It's completely up to you if you want to incorporate this into your reading system. Should charms land on or form a pattern along these lines, you can use the following meanings if and when you're pulled to do so:

One symbolizes something prime, important. Or a beginning, and the first key step. It's the path of the persona and self and the self's priorities: care, interest, discovery, focus, confidence, and empowerment. It's willful, unique, individual. It's the spark.

Two reveals the dynamics of a coupling. It can signify a union, commitment, or partnership; reciprocity and attraction or conflict and repulsion. It's duality, connection, and cooperation or a disconnect and opposition. It's an exchange, person to person, with balance or imbalance.

Three bears witness to both increase, expansion, and growth and loss and dishonesty. It's a three-way partnership or a third energy, the sum or result of a merging. It's also an addition, such as a child or a pet. Three can be a holy or unholy trinity: a third party that helps by lending support or hinders by interfering, meddling, or downright deceiving, such as in a love triangle. It can be a small wish come true. When auspicious, there's something extra, like part-time hours or passive income. When inauspicious, troubles add up; there's a worsening or difficulties that come from an outside source. As a herald of potential, there is small, step-by step progress up the ladder, but this warrants action and extra effort to reach the stability of four.

Four is stable, solid, even-tempered, four-walled, four-cornered, *four* better or worse, and brings the concept of foundation, structure, and stabilization.

Four is thickly rooted in the tangible, that which you can see, touch, and hold; it's squareness, anything with four corners, such as beds (sick, marriage, stranger's), buildings, institutions, documents, licenses, tables (work, social), desks, and plots of land. It also represents routine, the status quo and sameness, things that don't change. While four can be a fortress, a bastion of security that keeps things out, it can also be a prison or jail cell, a cage that confines. It's routine, the same old, same old, boredom, stagnation, or so down-to-earth that it clips your mercurial wings.

Five is kinetic, adventurous, and brings change—sometimes with chaos and conflict riding shotgun. It dislikes complacency. It also wants to be divine, honestly, and so it tests, pressures, and pushes something through the paces, like a quality-control check to see if any screws fall out or seams burst. And they do. But what does that tell you? Five offers an undercurrent of turbulence that challenges what you may be perceiving as stable and sure-footed. It could manifest as an argument or misunderstandings or escalate into a breakup or divorce, quitting a job or being fired.

Traditionally, five was also the number of the body, particularly the hand with its five fingers. In certain contexts, five expresses the channeling of this energy into something constructive such as craftsmanship, working with one's hands, labor or physical activity. When auspicious, it's the "hand of friendship" and the "right-hand" path, as the fair, truthful, and just way of doing things. When inauspicious, traditionally it's known as the "hand that holds the knife," which mostly implies cutting something or someone out of your life, or following the "left-hand" path of lies, bad choices, criminal behavior—not doing the right thing. It can also be adventure, a paradigm-breaker, short trips, itinerancy or the inability to settle down.

Six is the hour of Venus and connects with peace, harmony, aesthetics, beauty, the arts, and communication. Ruled by the heart and emotions, six radiates genuine warmth, kindness, compassion, and a purpose and spirit of helping others. It emphasizes a rich inner life and a compassionate and heart-centered hard-wiring, nurturing, and caretaking; it's the vibration of love. Six is the path of teachers, mentors, counselors, and those working with children, the disenfranchised, or the less fortunate. Organic and effortless, its energy feels innocent, sweet, childlike, less complicated, and without agenda. This can also be experienced as remembrance or nostalgia, a vague longing for something in the past that's passed through a filter of yearning.

Seven can be a tricky, layered, illusory, or consciously under-the-radar line. Lucky 7? Yes, that too, and it's luck that's been manifested through cause and effect, as in you create your own . . . This is the path of risk-taking, as well as any upturns or reversals of fortune. Expect the unexpected: surprises, setbacks, and outcomes that are considerably better or direr. Seven represents appetites, indulgences, desires: What do you want and what are you prepared to do to get it? It's also a path of deep mysticism and vision; it acknowledges and confirms the presence of spiritual, metaphysical, or paranormal experiences or gifts. It can also be a channel for nonform consciousness, messages from ancestors, or other spirit energy.

Eight involves others, but unlike three, it's a group dynamic, as in clubs, associations, colleagues and peers, roundtables, conferences, teams, or gangs. It represents coming together to raise cups, weddings, reunions, celebrations, or social engagements. Eight deals with assessing and balancing imbalance and stabilizing instability and so includes the scales of justice, law, medicine, emergency services, and counseling. It involves research, analysis, investigation, examinations and exams (academic and medical), and forensics or a forensic approach to solving a problem. Eight is also the number of "muchness": prosperity, abundance, money management, easy come and easy go, cycling, investments, numbers, counting and accounting, and resources. It can express the need for balancing the books, curtailing spending, economy, and rainy-day thinking. Eight is also linked to hoarders or the penny-pinching heart of a miser. Eight doesn't favor rash and impulsive action, but conversely embodies grift, hard and meticulous work, mastery, plodding, planning, determination, and doing something to get something done.

Nine connects to wisdom, higher learning, power, and raised consciousness. Self-discovery, mastery, and actualization all reside here. It's the path of those who are self-employed or rise to the top of their profession or calling. Nine embodies an ambition or experience of fame or infamy, renown, celebrity or notoriety. Dreams, goals, or wishes are either green-lighted and come true or remain unfulfilled. It's an ascent to or fall from grace. Nine also symbolizes space, time, and distance, something enduring or something delayed. It's also a pause, a time for eyes-wide-open reflection, correction, or change before something funnels into the completion of ten.

Ten carries the energy of completion. The cycle has ended; *finito la comedia,* show's over, the curtain's coming down; go home; tomorrow's another day—and you won't see yesterday again. It's the pinnacle, for better or for worse; there was a cause, but now *here's Johnny*—the effect, consequence, reward, or retribution. When you reduce the number 10 by adding the 1 and 0, you're left with the single number 1. This brings you full circle. In this respect, it represents a homecoming, a reboot. Charms that land on the ten line can herald or describe a straw that's breaking the camel's back, a deal-breaker. The message is, *It is what it is*; the question asked is, *How will you receive, process, release, or carry an event or experience forward?* Will you break or repeat the pattern? Look to ten for guidance.

Eleven is the enlightened path of the eternal self. The charms that fall on this line convey messages from Spirit that have to do with the soul's purpose, alignment, and evolution. Are you on the right path, making free-will choices that are attuned with your true north, or have you lost your bearings? Any shifts or changes indicated along this line may be out of your control and perhaps unwanted. Eleven says trust, reconnect with your faith, and know that you're being heavily guided by your spirit team along this path. You will come to understand this unequivocally.

Twelve is a path that changes the focus from the soul to the incarnated self—your spirit, that which animates our physical container—and how it's interacting with others. How are you developing, directing, expressing, using, honoring, and experiencing your energy and gifts? What makes you unique? How are you embracing this divine individuality? How is it being shared, and what is its impact on others? While one is a function of the will, twelve embodies the creative spirit and spark in action. It can provide valuable insight on what's being attracted based on the dynamics revealed along this path.

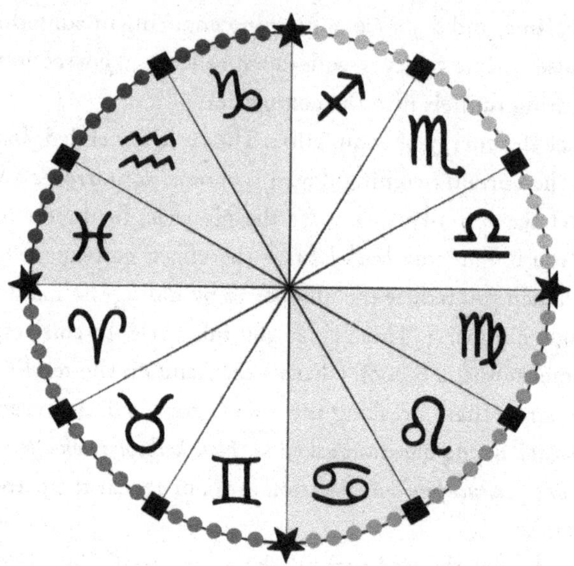

Castrology: Keywords for the Twelve Houses of the Zodiac

Divide your charmala into the twelve houses of the zodiac wheel. (The first house, ruled by Aries sits between 9 and 8 o'clock, and your houses will progress counterclockwise.) Charge each segment with the traits that correspond to the astrological house meanings. When charms land in these houses, you'll be able to blend the core meanings of the charms with these energized areas. If you're an avid astrologer, you can also use the date ranges governing the signs to help predict timings.

Here's a greenback starter kit of keywords.

First House ruled by Aries:

Self. Projected persona. How you're seen by others. Attitude. Chutzpah.

Second House ruled by Taurus:

What we have: money, material possessions, and goods. Working for a living. Values. Security.

Third House ruled by Gemini:

The intellect. Thinking. Understanding. Investigating. Questioning. Learning. Communication. News and messages. Siblings. Neighbors. Early education. Short trips.

Fourth House ruled by Cancer:

Hearth and home. Family. Roots of origin. Settling. Mother's imprint.

Fifth House ruled by Leo:

Self-expression. Creativity. Romance. Short-term relationships and affairs. Pleasure. Play, recreation, hobbies. Entertainment. Theater and drama. Children.

Sixth House ruled by Virgo:

Health and wellness. Nutrition. Fitness. Self-care. Usefulness and service. How we like to do things: analysis, daily grind, routines, and organization. Pets.

Seventh House ruled by Libra:

Union. Close relationships and partnerships. Known or open enemies. Conflicts with others; theft. Marriage. Engagement. Contracts. Legal issues.

Eighth House ruled by Scorpio:

Intense. Sex. Death. Transformation. Initiation. Taxes. Other people's property and money: real estate, investments, and inheritances.

Ninth House ruled by Sagittarius:

Long-distance travel. Adventure. Foreign lands. Spirituality and religion. Philosophy. Core ideals. Belief systems. Politics. Publishing. Higher education. Luck. Risk. Chance.

Tenth House ruled by Capricorn:

Status. Reputation. Vocation. Vision. Fame. Honors. Achievement. Tradition. Authority. Corporations. Structure and boundaries. Discipline. Father's imprint. Note: charms that fall on the cusp of the tenth house (also the twelve path) can reveal insight into career path.

Eleventh House ruled by Aquarius:

Social life. Friendship. Groups. Community. Enjoying the fruits of labor. Altruism, charity, and humanitarian pursuits. Turning dreams and goals into reality. Focus on the future. Technology. The internet. Networking. Science. Astrology. Numbers and data. Revolution. Innovation. Eccentricity.

Twelfth House ruled by Pisces:

Transcendence. Final phases toward completion. Old age. Release. Surrender. Secrets. Addictions and self-sabotage. Institutions, prisons, hospitals, and asylums. Isolation and confinement. Hidden agendas and enemies. The psyche. Unconscious drivers. Psychic ability.

Cast Away

TECHNIQUE

Amok! Amok! Amok!
—from *Hocus Pocus* (1993)

We're just throwing things onto a flat surface. What could possibly go wrong? Well, that's an easy one: What goes up must come down. How your pieces depart, drop, and disperse across your surface can deepen or dampen the quality of a reading. Casting is a daring act of mise-en-scène, like positioning actors—your glorious cast of curios—on the stage—your reading surface. Obviously, you're divining, not directing, so once your pieces take off and offer a brief *nod to the gods*, you have no more control before gravity takes over.

Your charms will either find a meaningful place in a sacred composition or, heaven help you, land miles away from one another, flee the scene entirely, or pile up in an uninspired lump. Candidly, it really doesn't matter how you get your ensemble to hit their marks as long as the casting consistently supports your method of interpretation and reduces wear and tear on the more delicate members, of which, inevitably, you'll have a few. Some of the factors that greatly increase an ideal dispersion are height, the timing of the release, and touch. Adopt and practice a style that encourages a pleasing charmscape: that reasonable arrangement of pieces that promotes—and permits—your best interpretation. Here are a few tips to help you choose a style and refine the technique of the toss.

The One-Off: This is an ideal method for quick pulls and direct messages. Randomly pick one charm from your container—or a very few. Then pick another—or few more. Repeat. Should you ever need more clarity, backstory, or detail on a specific part of a larger reading, set up a bracelet beside your casting and use this technique to conduct a follow-up question and answer.

The Swirl and Flick: If, by the way, you store your charms in a box or tin, you may want to transfer them to a bowl before every casting. This stops charms from hiding out in the four corners and ducking out of the range of your sweeping fingers. Swirlers and flickers use their dominant hand to spin their pieces clockwise in a bowl until they feel ready to stop and pinch a few. Then, in one deft and fluid motion, they gently flick them onto their surface. If you're doing any magical or spiritual work involving the shadow, release, or cleansing, use your nondominant hand and swirl the charms widdershins, or counterclockwise.

Sprinkling, Salt and Peppering: Have you ever watched a chef season their food? They're not just chucking seasoning willy-nilly—too much here, not enough there. Their heads are bowed, their fingers pulsing with intention, and they're actively focused on a result. That's a great way to add trinkets, trifles, baubles, and bits into a divination.

Also, in the same way a chef finishes a plate with olive oil, placing their thumb over the bottle opening to reduce the flow to a mindful drizzle, you can sprinkle a few drops of an all-natural cologne like Kananga Water into the bowl before a reading. Then get your hands and energy in there. Be soft, but don't be shy. Go right down to the bottom and along the sides. Focus on the sound created by your choir of charms. It can be a bit jarring and full of tension. When you can *connect with* the harmony in that cacophony, you'll know you're both ready to go.

How many charms should you cast? There's no right or wrong—just scale. If you're doing a small casting, one fingerful will suffice. If you're going deeper or looking for multiple layers or storylines, two fingerfuls provide plenty of insight. From a height of one or two inches above your surface, sprinkle or salt and pepper your charms over your surface. Imbue your fingers with the duty of care, instructing your pieces to form a workable charmscape.

The Out-You-Go or Dump and Clump: This is an unceremonious evacuation of things from where they once were to where they're about to go—voted the most likely to cause a mound of a virtually unreadable mess. You may be able to carve out meanings from a few pieces that are clinging together for dear life, but typically what happens is that those poor castmates who took the time and care to show up get overwhelmed and lost in the chaos. The result of which, invariably, is that you, the hopeful caster, succumb to hopelessness. In this tragic instance, let's defer to the wisdom of a great poet:

> *Let there be spaces in your togetherness.*
> *And let the winds of the heavens dance between you.*
> —Kahlil Gibran, *The Prophet*

The Toss-Up: Experienced bone readers can masterfully toss a bowlful of pieces up and onto a mat and get the distribution right every time. How? Practice, focus, Spirit. If your set is mostly comprised of larger objects, by all means, perfect this technique. But for my kitsch casters who are working predominantly with Wee Ones, salt and peppering will give you the best control and protection against loss and breakage.

Random vs. Preselection

There are two ways to pick pieces in a divination: one invokes a supernatural force, and the other involves conscious intention. Random selection is the magical act of intuitively choosing the pieces that want to present. This is the go-to method for most divinations. Preselection, on the other hand, is where you sort through your kit searching for a specific piece. *Whoop-dee-do*, you say. *Where's the fun in that?* You may not want to do this for every casting; however, this technique is a way of ensuring that you have on-topic pieces. You would preselect a symbol to represent your perception of a subject or idea, and in doing so, you're saying, *Let's be clear: we're* going *to be talking about this!* And now you can randomly select charms to cast around or with your preselected pieces. How they all land and combine will always open up new and unexpected dialogues.

A combination of random and preselection can give you added control over the parameters of a reading. It's a very happy marriage. Here's how this works:

Sample question: *What can I expect if I leave my current job to become a professional reader in the next three to six months?*

Find and preselect two charms: one for your work and another for your dream goal. An American penny has two sides, which can be for your current job: heads is Lincoln's profile portrait (your boss) and tails could be the Lincoln Memorial, scenes from Lincoln's life, or the Union shield, depending on what year the penny was minted (the physical workplace). Maybe you have a witch's hat charm that can symbolize a career in divination. You could simply, just preselect then cast the penny and the witch's hat, then sprinkle charms over and around them, but let's crank up the stakes a little.

Why not preselect additional charms to represent **yes** (go; do this; it will happen), **no** (stop, fuhgeddaboudit), and **maybe** (delay, something needs to happen before your wish is fulfilled). Place all of these pieces in a **blind bowl**, a small bowl used as a temporary holding facility, like a green room for charms awaiting their close-ups. Now *randomly* select a pinch of charms and add these to the bowl. When you are ready, pour them into your palm, and, eyes closed, do your best to gently disperse and direct all of these charms into a horizontal line.

When you're ready, find the **look-at-me** charms: the coin and the witch's hat. Now begin a long line of internal questioning. What order have they landed in? Time travels from left to right, so think of far left as the past (that which is consciously known) and far right as the future (the unknown). Decide what it will mean if charms land above or below the line. *What's not falling into place? What commentary's being delivered from the sidelines?* If the witch's hat is far left, and the coin (tails side up) is far right, it's acknowledging your goal but saying that you'll still have your day job moving ahead. The wider the gap between these two charms, in that order, the more your current reality displaces the dream. And which side of the coin presented: the boss or the workplace? What if the coin lands Lincoln side up (boss) and to the left? Should other charms support this narrative, maybe in three to six months you'll have a change of your day job or boss. What if the two key pieces are stacked? Which piece is on top? The best place for the witch's hat to be is to the right of the coin, near or at the end of your line and touching an auspicious charm, such as yes, money, change, reputation, or transformation. Where and how have the yes, no, and maybe pieces landed? Are there charms between the coin and the witch's hat? What could they be saying? Are they suggesting actionable steps or presenting details that contribute to a timeline of how and when your dream goal can be realized?

Word Up: Beaded Letter Chains

The VIP kit is one way to introduce key life areas and hot topics into a divination without having to rely on illustrations on a casting surface. But there's another. It's a versatile, superfun, ready for any context, castable DIY tool: word chains.

A few years ago, I was about to do a casting that involved lots of contributing factors, a real estate decision, the prospect of retirement, as well as the stability of a marriage. There were a few parties involved, two addresses, and a few unexpressed side concerns. Alrighty then. While contemplating my approach, I remembered a thrift store find. It was a small, plastic box filled with a few beaded ball chains and square *A–Z* letter beads. This adorable DIY kit was designed so that you could snap your name around the stem of a wineglass. So I began customizing castable word chains that identified the parties, different houses, and key actions or decisions, e.g., *retire.* It would be a breakthrough technique that added clarity, control, color, and a whole new degree of predictive accuracy into my castings.

Like preselecting specific charms, word chains are look-at-me pieces with a set intention: *one way or another—we're dealing with this.* When using word chains to represent key people, concepts, or details, you're also keeping all of your charms in play. Now that reclining deck chair, for example, that means retirement can also present randomly. Anytime multiple pieces with shared meanings appear, you have much stronger validation for your messaging and also the possible presentation of a theme. Plus, word chains can touch, completely obscure and block, support or wrap around or contain charms, adding nuance. Once you're done with your reading, you have a choice. You can either release the letters back into their box or build and keep specialty kits in their own tiny tins.

We're going to have such fun!

Word Chain Checklist

- ☐ Bulk 6 mm cube *A–Z* acrylic letter beads. Ensure the holes are approximately 3.4 mm/0.13 inch because anything smaller fits elastic string, but not the thickness of a small beaded chain. Additionally, look for a good color contrast: white on black, black on white, or neon-colored print on black. It makes reading the letters printed on all four sides much easier.
- ☐ 6 mm acrylic, mixed cubes, 0–9 number beads. Large hole and good contrast. Numbers are useful should you want to differentiate locations by their street address. Some house or building numbers are simple; others can be longer and could involve duplicates, which is why I keep three sets of 0–9 beads.

- ☐ Metal ball bead chains with connector clasps (approx. 12 cm). They come in a range of bold colors.
- ☐ Small tins or storage containers for themed word-chain kits. Labels or stickers.

Working with Word Chains

The mini word chain base kit: Be prepared. You can create custom castable words and numbers on the spot. When your reading is over, unsnap (physically and energetically) these chains, and mix the beads back in with the rest. Always have a tin filled with a few chains, two sets of *A–Z* letter beads with extra vowels, three sets of numbers 0–9, and, if you have them, a few hearts.

Hearts? Yes, some letter bead kits come with hearts or other symbols. Marking the beginning of key or longer words with a heart makes it easier to identify in a pinch. Hearts also make good replacement vowels. Always looking to economize on vowels, I use **XXX** for my ***no*** (avoid this) word chains and three hearts for ***yes*** (thumbs-up).

Create a specialty word chain kit: Create a themed kit for specific daily, general, or context-driven divinations and keep this handy in its own cute, labeled container.

SAMPLE THEMES FOR WORD CHAIN KITS

- Rise and Shine: Daily
- General
- Manifestation
- Love, Romance, and Relationships
- Self-Care
- Animal Communication

- Yes or No
- Sports
- Alignment

Word of the Day: Creating a Rise and Shine Casting Kit

Description: Used for a quick daily casting that reveals a key theme, challenge, or opportunity and then helps you seize the day.

Notes: Add two small dice: a context and an advice die. Roll the context die to frame the setting; then, the other for advice. (See chapter 13 for a few dicier divinations).

DICE NUMBER MEANINGS

1. Self. Beginnings. Solitary.
2. Relationship. Commitments.
3. Creativity. Growth. Expansion.
4. Stability. Structure. Status Quo. Manifestation or completion.
5. Conflict.
6. Harmony. Resolution. Victory.

Word Chains and Keyword Meanings

Earth: tangible, mundane, health, home, finances, construction

Air: intellect, mental pursuits, psychology, challenges, decisions

Fire: ambition, passion, will, action, determination, perseverance

Water: emotion, sensation, indulgence, creativity, arts, beauty, self-care

Spirit: spirituality, highest-good message

XXX: no, heads-up, red flag, alarm, avoid this, incoming issue, bad energy

♥♥♥ : (if you don't have hearts, use three *Ys*) yes, good energy, stabilizes or mitigates anything inauspicious, do this

---

Scribble

When building word chains, keep your words as short as possible or use abbreviations. When cast, they'll combine and intertwine with charms, and the letters will splay. You might have to take a second to identify the word. And sometimes, the letters do strange things. They can form their own two or three-letter message. With practice, you'll get to know your chains, but it helps to give them a brief review before a reading. You can always color code the chains for easier recognition, such as red for fire, brown for earth, blue for water, white for air, purple for spirit.

The Mixed Media Divination

Before you embark on your day, focus on an intention for the reading, then try this quick forecast with word chains, base kit charms, and dice. You have a couple of options:

Preselect your word chains. Lay them out on your cloth, however you like, then cast over them. This approach broadens the scope of a reading.

Or try this:

For a blind bowl: Randomly select just a few word chains from your themed kit. Add a small pinch of charms, maybe a VIP. Then cast them all onto your surface. Use this approach to divine something more targeted.

A Sample Mixed Media Casting: What's the Best Use of My Day?

Context die: Four

Chains: *SPIRIT* and *AIR*

Charms: Alice in Wonderland (with her Drink Me bottle) and Gingerbread House

Advice die: Four

Two fours. Clearly this will be a routine day where both the atmosphere and advice favor stability and responsibility. The fours can also be alluding to something with four corners—such as a building or desk. Mind and Spirit factor prominently. Gingerbread House is my charm of sanctuary, and it falls in the middle of the *AIR* word chain. The *I* in the word *AIR* has isolated. It falls to the right. Today's "adventure" (Alice) is solitary and involves staying indoors, at my desk, focused on an intellectual pursuit (which is also spiritual in nature). Alice's back is turned to the *SPIRIT* chain. Too much time sequestered in my head often results in a disconnect from some healthful, highest-good choices (like moving, eating, or hydrating). There's strong advice here that says balance is best achieved by metaphorically "drinking the potion" which, it occurs, allows Alice access to the garden. So remember to take breaks, go outside, breathe, and get out of your head for a bit.

Creating a Love, Romance, and Relationships Word Chain Kit

Description: Used for a quick casting aimed at revealing the dynamics of a current relationship (friendly, romantic, business or with self), then helping you process, clarify, and make empowered choices.

Notes: Dice optional. Add a red heart or another piece symbolizing passion. Wherever it lands, it augments a message or indicates where your will or desires are most passionately engaged. If you get a pair of chains falling together—fire (active), water (passive), air (active), or earth (passive)—you can incorporate this additional layer: read their *elemental dignities.* A very basic rule of thumb: Fire and water don't get along and weaken each other; Air and earth—same thing. Mostly, the other combinations intensify or support each other.

WORD CHAIN CHECKLIST WITH KEYWORD MEANINGS

Note: Use hearts or other symbols to separate a compound word, e.g., *let♥go.*

- ☐ ***Self:*** main significator
- ☐ ***Other:*** secondary significator
- ☐ (Don't forget, you can also make individual name chains.)
- ☐ ***Attract:*** short for *attraction.* Can also provide a spiritual message on what sort of experiences or people you're attracting and why.
- ☐ ***Nature:*** character, personality, traits
- ☐ ***Earth:*** physicality, financial, reliable, boring, athletic
- ☐ ***Air:*** intellect, psychology, ruled by reason, divorce, widow
- ☐ ***Water:*** emotions, indulgence, compassion, family-oriented, artistic, moody
- ☐ ***Fire:*** gregarious, ambitious, attention-seeking, passionate, fiery, leadership
- ☐ ***Spirit:*** highest-good message; faith or belief system
- ☐ ***Lesson:*** what wants to be learned
- ☐ ***Pattern:*** something with repetition, what wants to be broken or healed
- ☐ ***S(elf)-care or ♥-care:*** self-love, making yourself a priority—you need to love yourself first.
- ☐ ***Let-go:*** an attachment to a person, belief, or behavior that's no longer useful

- ☐ ***Ideal:*** a message reminding you of a personal core ideal. Are you honoring it? If not, why not?
- ☐ ***Perfect:*** What's perfect? Or, perhaps, *everything* is perfect: Are you getting what you've really consciously or unconsciously asked for? Some sitters say they want to be in a relationship, yet confess that they avoid all efforts to meet anyone. This is why their choice to remain single, until they shift an unconscious intention, is perfect.
- ☐ ***Act:*** also short for *activate.* What action wants to be either tabled or pursued?
- ☐ ***Belief:*** What we believe, we become. What message are you putting out to the universe?
- ☐ ***Align:*** short for *alignment.* Your true north, the true you, the path to wish fulfillment.
- ☐ ***XXX:*** no, heads-up, red flag, alarm, avoid this, incoming issue, bad energy
- ☐ ♥♥♥ (if you don't have hearts, use three *Y*s): yes, good energy, stabilizes or mitigates anything inauspicious; do this
- ☐ ***Trigger:*** stimulus that provokes a reactionary response, anger, potential conflict, a need for a contemplative pause
- ☐ ***Choice:*** a message involving a key decision, cause and effect
- ☐ ***Event:*** Could mean a date or timing, or an invitation, an occurrence or group event.
- ☐ ***Love:*** The charm that lands with this chain will speak volumes about the dynamic of a relationship. May the red heart fall here for you every time!
- ☐ ***Heat:*** What's escalating or wants more energy?
- ☐ ***Ice:*** What's cooling or wants less passion or engagement?

GRIMOIRE PROMPT

DESIGN YOUR OWN WORD CHAIN KIT

Theme: ______________________

Description: ______________________

____

Notes: ______________________

____

____

____

____

____

Word Chains and Keyword Meanings: ______________________

____

____

____

____

____

____

____

____

____

The Casting Kit and Kaboodle Checklist

If you find yourself getting lost or blessedly distracted by the magnitude of your casting kit and kaboodle, you're not alone. When I work, I have to remind myself to stop goofing around and keep it simple and organized. Never happens. This is why you may also want to immortalize your sacred gear with a grimoire entry. Mine looks something like this:

Charms, base kit: Bagged inside a tin lunch box shaped like a guitar case. (I'm my own roadie.) Although, they may be moving to a roomier GhostStop equipment case.

VIPs (roomy zippered makeup bag).

Specialty kits: letters, numbers and chains, dice, astrological charms

Specialty decks: Symbol-rich tarot decks that layer well with charms and oracle decks with word prompts for free association work

Themed word chain kits: Base kit (general), Yes/No, Manifestation and Alignment, Rise and Shine, Daily, and Football. These are kept in their own tiny tins.

Charmalas and matching seer's eyes: These are additional bracelets for side or timeline work.

Cloths: vintage, solid-colored cotton and cloths; black leather

Fave pointer(s): vintage knitting needles; light-up chopsticks, crystal cocktail stirrers

Four bowls: base kit charms, VIPs, word chains, blind bowl

Casting grimoire: A-5 binder-style. Zippered pockets store sets of index cards (including astrological houses; numbered paths; and dice cheat notes), as well as folded lace handkerchiefs.

Spa products: Kananga and Florida water; charcoal soap

Personal must-haves: A loupe or reading glasses; candle and lighter; lip gloss

The Calm Before the Casting

SACRED SPACE AND MINDSET

Imagination is the beginning of creation. You imagine what you desire, you will what you imagine, and at last, you create what you will.
—George Bernard Shaw

Sacred Space: Creating a Parlor of One's Own

Don't be shy—come on in. Welcome to my gracious parlor. Make yourself at home. There's a crackling fire in the stone hearth to take the chill out of the damp night air. And a cozy Queen Anne chair with a plump pillow. Rest by the fire and watch plummy raindrops pelt against the lead-paned windows. I know you don't startle easily, but my, how those tree limbs beat and scrape against the glass, as if trying to either wake the dead . . . or herald their arrival. To some, this tempestuous weather might seem frightful, but we, kindred in spirit, answer the call to a higher and deeper understanding and rub our hands together in electric joy. We drink in this charged atmosphere because, dear Magical One, this is when and where we do our best work.

In an ideal world, we'd all have this special place, or what author Virginia Woolf called *a room of one's own*. Wouldn't it be glorious to have an actual office with a door that shuts (tightly) keeping out anyone or anything daring to disrupt our creative or magical process. Imagine! This would be the room, *our* room, where we'd go to think, be calm, meditate, or breathe; where we'd meet and greet our ancestors and helping spirits and set up altars to honor them. We don't care about Muggle things in here: the remote control be damned. We mindfully manage the atmosphere in this room, keeping out drama, toxicity, and chaos and maintaining a high vibration so we can be the clearest possible channel for our work.

And, just a thought: maybe we'd have cabinets filled with oddities, candles, crystals, herbs, tarot and oracle cards, vials, oils, crows, frogs—and books, books, glorious books. And let's not forget some apothecary jars filled with gummy bears, lemon drops, or chocolate? What if this room were in a house that sat high on a hill and overlooked a centuries-old cemetery? Or on a lake or a farm with a spectacular view of cows and a spectacular sunrise or sunset? Wouldn't that be dreamy? Well, yes it would . . . but let's float back down to reality. What if you don't have that physical space within your residence in which to work? What can you do? *More than you think.* Where can you go? *Farther yet much closer than you imagine.*

Let's go find your own personal spirit room. This is a destination, a meditative space where you can go to meet your guides and helping spirits and, on occasion, spend some quality time with your beloved ancestors. With a little practice, you'll be able to get there quicker and stay longer.

Close your eyes. Take a few deep breaths. Let your mind's eye roam beyond the confines of your present environment. What do you see? Limitless, isn't it just? Here, in this expanse of velvety darkness, lies prime psychic real estate, within which you can begin to create then decorate an energetic space. You alone have the key that can unlock doors inside of your own liminal landscape. Use it to access an expansive new dimension that's encrypted with your soul's code.

If you're new to meditation and visualization, in the beginning it's perfectly fine to allow your conscious mind and imagination to define that space. Hang a curtain here. Put a stained-glass window there. Think of it like an astral getaway, a bunkie for your Higher Self. If you like, go online or flip through books or magazines to help you personalize your spirit room. What about a water fountain? Perhaps a horsehair couch or a harvest table where you can invite your ancestors and helping spirits to come, sit, have a chat, and help you work? Eventually, the more times you enter this space, new things—furniture, orchards, fields, hallways, flowers, windows, animals—will begin appearing on their own without any invested effort. Trust these developments. See and honor them as signs that new channels are opening. You can build your spirit room *any* way that your heart desires. Make it a safe space surrounded by the angelic forces of light. Set intentions that only the vibration of love may enter. With repetition, trust, and faith, you'll be able to move into this calm, high-vibrational, meditative, receptive yet protected space within minutes before every casting.

Tip: If you're a fan of soft background music or sound while you work, try searching YouTube on your phone, tablet, or computer for atmospheric rooms. Sure, silence is golden, but never underestimate the sublime ambience of a thunderstorm, medieval tavern, dark academic library, summer kitchen, Victorian parlor, crackling fire, blizzard, rustling autumn leaves, or boiling cauldrons to energize your space and put a howling wind behind your sails.

Ritual: A Divine Opening Act

Creatures of habit, we're used to performing our own series of ritualized acts every day—some at a specific time or in an order that somehow makes sense in the moment. Wake up. (Always a good thing). Java first. (Sacrosanct.) Jabber later. (Much later). Breakfast. Crossword puzzle? Check weather and messages. A book before bed. As ordinary as these may seem, don't kid yourself—they're ceremonial. These little performances require attention to detail and focus, and so lend structure and some semblance of control and context to our hectic and often unpredictable lives. And most importantly, they require us to be purposeful and present. So you see? You're already used to this idea of ritual and ready to do something special before setting the Wee Ones free on an unsuspecting surface.

Before you begin any kind of spiritual work, creating and observing a meaningful routine will only enrich your sacred practice. Like a plane taxiing on the runway, you're preparing to take flight into the otherworldly. Allowing that time to enact a ritual before a casting helps raise your vibration so that you can shift consciousness from the guarded, closed, and mundane to the ecstatic, receptive, and mystical. It's also an expression of humility and respect for your craft and discipline, as well as your hardworking spirit team. It doesn't have to be elaborate. An intentional act of lighting a candle and the humble offer of a few words of prayer are seen and heard. Your precasting ritual—whatever you say or do and how you find the eye of your own hurricane—will be a deeply personal affair. It's a divine reflection of your direction as a reader.

When you think about it, rituals are the graceful process of harmonizing your outer and inner sanctums. Once you develop your own system and method of casting, you'll get to know your must-have tools and trimmings and how you want everything arranged. Savor the setup, the mindful shuffling of stuff. Aesthetics play a big role in our fun and fine divining experiences, so surround yourself with whatever resonates with your soul style. There's nothing like getting *the call* to a well-appointed table.

Some casters prefer consistency. Their system is stationary, and for either personal or logistical reasons, it remains the same. I've always liked Martha Stewart's philosophy on home entertaining—that rediscovery of setting, favorite things, tastes, and ideas. Why not let the context of the reading occasionally inform the setup, table, casting cloth, tools, bowls, crystals, figurines, candles, and curios?

Once the table's laid, it's time to head inward. Put your phone on airplane mode. Now, behind closed eyes, you begin that journey into your sacred space. Be selfishly selfless. Bye-bye distraction. Arrivederci stress. These are a few ritualistic acts that might warm the way into your ready-set-throw tradition.

Magic fingers: Rub your hands together until you can feel the energy rise, pulse, and spark through your fingertips. Palms outward, riffle your fingertips, in a witchy come-hither manner. Now, select your charms.

Spirit rattle: Cup your charmala in your hands and shake it gently. When you feel a shift in energy, you'll know you're ready. Now it can be formed into a circle over your casting surface. If, by the way, you'd like to incorporate even more sound, you can thread mini bells into your beaded strand.

Table manners: Some casters set up ancestral offerings on their table—a treat, a small glass of water, or sometimes even a stronger spirit. If this sounds like something you'd like to do, just remember to never consume any food or drink that venerates the dead. Dispose of it as part of your post-casting grounding ritual, and toss it outside while saying thanks and farewell.

Closed for business: When you finish a larger casting, don't forget to close your space and ground. Snuff out your candle and find the best and easiest way to return to the earthly realm and ground. Go outside, if you can. Eat something yummy—and hydrate.

Balancing Acts

There's a sacred but tenuous marriage between the mundane and the magical. As a fully functional and attuned diviner, it's sensible to maintain a healthy balance between the two. Too much fairy dust and unicorn incontinence and your guidance could lack the experiential grounding that makes you a relatable authority for what you preach. Likewise, commit to a low-vibrational, projection-based comfort zone, and your craft will be mired in the muck. No liftoff for you—or, more importantly, your sitters. An honest but kind knowledge of self, combined with a dedicated ritual of self-care and constant self-reflection, will always hold you in good stead. No one said it would be easy. But it's a beautiful path we get to walk. And oh, the splendiferous light at the end of this tunnel.

Practice, embrace, and hold sacred the ritualistic and therapeutic habits in your life that raise you up—no matter what anyone else thinks. If that means getting your hands into soil, cuddling with a fur baby, listening to music, feeding the birds, throwing paint at a canvas, lighting a candle at breakfast during a rainstorm, eating Moon Cheese, baking bread or cookies—just do it. And keep doing it.

Mystic Molly Maid: Cleaning Your Magical Space

It's much easier to maintain positive energy in a room of one's own where you can control who or what comes in. But if your workspace is shared, it can inadvertently play host to life's inevitable demands and dramas: everything from someone else's possessions, thoughts, and emotions to sounds, choice of language, and behavior can leave an energetic imprint, heavy, tense, lethargic, or nauseating. And—heaven forfend—you're a wide-open empath who, like a two-ply paper towel, cleanses objects, people, and places by absorbing and storing their psychic mess.

The healthiest way to restore positivity and raise the vibration in a space is to become your own Mystic Molly Maid. Naturally, good-old elbow grease, sweeping, scrubbing, dusting, and decluttering (whistling while you work) will always improve the balance and flow of energy in a room, but, unless you're Cinderella, who has time for that? There are many magical products that you can use to shift stuck energy, lighten, balance, and galvanize the feel of a room. When a tool whispers, calls, or shouts at you, trust your intuition. A little spritz of your favorite potion? Why not? It's also aromatherapeutic and refreshing. At times, I've been drawn to cleansing with smoke by burning a stick of fragrant and irresistible palo santo. Or I've ignited dried herbs or resins in a mini cauldron before directing lower-vibrational energy out of an open window or door. On occasion, I've used an antique handbell. Its ring is crystal clear, high-pitched, and tenacious, and it performs like the spiritual version of an industrial degreaser. Then there's the choir of singing bowls with soft mallets that come in a range of sizes and chakra-healing frequencies. But for those pesky, hard-to-remove energetic stains, there's nothing quite like the sonorous Tibetan tingshas. The room becomes so shiny I can practically see myself. Still, what if you don't have any of these things at home? Should you wait to do a casting? Absolutely *not.*

Keep in mind, anything—no matter what the label claims—is just a thing, until you imbue it with intention. That's what transforms it into a sacred tool. I use palo santo in my precasting space cleansing because I adore the smell. It relaxes and enlivens me. I want it. It's a beloved part of my ritual—but I don't need it. I also always have lip gloss on my table. That's equally magical because I command it, and so, it must be. Everything you really need to work with energy—to shift, remove, raise, or transmute it—lies within you. It's all right there, behind closed eyes, curled up in a luminous ball, purring and ready to pounce on command. It's in you.

Let's go find it . . .

Sit down comfortably. Plant both feet firmly on the floor. Envision roots growing from the bottom of your feet and burrowing down into the cool, rich, fragrant earth. Breathe in through your nose. Hold. Exhale through your mouth. Repeat as many times as it takes to slow down your heart rate.

Imagine a beam, a pillar of brilliant white light that enters through the top of your head. Let it course through your core, flowing through every extremity, soothing and cleansing aches, pains, blockages, and worries.

Visualize this light now, like spent bathwater, pooling at your feet before filtering down through your roots, back into the dark, rich earth where it can be purified. In this new transmuted state, draw it back up. Allow the light that flows down from the universe to merge with the radiant stream that rises from the earth. Feel it strengthening within. Expand it outward and visualize it surrounding you with the vibration of love. Savor the lightness and brightness of your being, and give thanks. Slowly open your eyes. You're ready to work the room.

Lift your hands slightly and turn your palms outward. Take a few deep calming breaths. Now, walk around your space and feel into it. Is it tranquil? Is it giving you happy vibes? What emotions, senses, or thoughts are being evoked? Do they belong to you? If not and something feels funky, you can raise the energy and clear your space without any tools.

If there's an area of blocked or unstable energy, visualize it as a form and mentally throw a *cloak* over it. Visualize tendrils of light descending from the heavens and begin swirling, circling, then tightening around the unwanted energy. See those spirals of light remove and carry the form away and back into the universe where it can be blessed and transmuted.

Take a beat. Breathe and feel into the space again. Can you sense a difference? Finish your ritual by ceremonially laying hands over the area and sending love and a blessing to all concerned.

Superstition and Misfortune Tellers: Leaning into Fear

What falls to the floor comes to the door. Yikes.

Black cats. They're bad. The number 13. That's bad. Breaking mirrors. That's really bad. Like, seven years of bad. (Wearing white shoes after Labor Day—inexcusably bad.) Don't you just love a good ol' superstition, and the threat of unavoidable, imminent, or long-lasting misfortune? It gets your blood curdling and makes you feel half-alive.

Albeit quaint, these superstitions are examples of folk knowledge. As diviners, we hear a lot of them. For instance, here's one: anything that falls to the floor is coming to your door. All good if it's *the winner, winner, chicken dinner* oracle, but what if it's a coffin, cross, or a powerful enemy piece? What then?

Think of a charm or card you don't like.

How does this make you feel? *Apprehensive? Anxious?*

What's suddenly changed in your physiology? *Are you dizzy? Are you tense?*

If so, then this is a classic fear response and also a wonderful opportunity to talk about a huge elephant in the diviner's room. What if when you're reading, you draw something that you perceive as "unlucky" or menacing? Is there an able and ready fear body being activated? Have your thoughts instantly turned dark? Are you cursed? Is *catastrophe, unwanted change,* or *abandonment* typing your address into its GPS and making a beeline for your life?

We all know what happens next. Unless we're hardwired like the delightfully macabre Wednesday Addams (who sees a potential harbinger of disaster and thinks, *AWESOME!*), our sensible and sensitive stomachs fill with black adders, our palms begin to sweat, and we assume the brace position: put your hands over your crown chakra and place your third eye on your knees; slump forward and roll into an Armageddon ball. An excellent position from which to divine, right? Wrong.

As a diviner, please know that fear is *not* your friend. It's a very common evolutionary response for both beginner and seasoned readers alike, because we're all human and respond to a perceived threat the exact same way.

It begins in the mind.

A message is sent (via the Four Horsemen of the Apocalypse) to the central nervous system. Then our bodies release the hounds—cortisol and adrenaline—and we prepare for the Dance of Doom: fight-or-flight. What to do? What to do? It's so hard to decide on one or the other under such mind-warping duress.

Once triggered, the difference between some beginners and seasoned, in-the-trenches diviners is the ability to *stop* the circus from coming to town. While it's true that not every message or intuitive hit will be love and light and warm fuzzies, while you're in the vice grips of a fear response, your vibration plummets. Fear strangles, confuses, and obfuscates—that's its job. Your gig, however, is to fly above the storm clouds and turbulence where your connection to Spirit is as pure as possible. How else can you divine an answer, solution, or acceptance? No way you'll be able to discern the difference between an imagined or genuine Spirit-led message if you're stuck in the mind mud. The messenger can't be overstimulated and pretzeled with dread.

Spiritually speaking, fear is tricky. It's a highly kinetic energy with the power of self-fulfilling prophecy or the ability to attract that which, ironically, you fear the most. Imagine, you're wearing white and en route to an Italian restaurant—you know where I'm heading with this, right? You know what they say: Fortune favors the brave. The more self-possessed you are with that fork full of tomato sauce, the less likely you are to return home looking like a crime scene. And even if you do manage to splash some tasty, bright red marinara on your shirt, oh well. A balanced, in-the-moment, "Que Sera, Sera" attitude mitigates the enormity of minor events that we tend to supersize by worry. Your best defense is always a mindful offense: positivity.

Whenever one of your least favorite charms "falls to the floor" eliciting a strong personal reaction, see it as useful information, usually about something internal rather than external. But you won't know for sure unless you work through the fear body. It's a symbol that wants to engage and convey a message, and your best path to the truth will come from leaning into this fear response and letting it inform you about any old and limiting beliefs that need to be addressed and cracks in your auric armor that want to be healed and sealed.

And as for any scary, folked-up superstitions, treat them like baker's yeast. In order for anything to rise or manifest, it needs to be fed the sugar of a lower-vibrational belief. So: *Don't. Feed. It.*

Leaning into Fear

The goal of the following exercise is to identify, demystify, and then show fear who's boss.

Sort through your charms and pull out three that trigger the heebie-jeebies. Journeying with these symbols can help you open a dialogue with your unconscious. In this exercise, we're going to work with your metaphoric understanding of a symbol and deepen a connection to that charm's healing potential.

GRIMOIRE PROMPT

Grab your casting grimoire. And let's do this for three charms:

The charm: ______________________
Sample: *The coffin*

Describe it in the first five words that come to you off the top of your head. The ________________ is ______________, ______________, ________________, ________________, and ________________.
Sample: *Black. Closed. Permanent. Grief. Unexpected.*

Review. Which, if any, of these descriptive words feels charged or the most personal?____________________. Circle or highlight the word.
Sample: *Permanent. Unexpected.*

When I see, touch, or connect to this charm, I feel ____________________.
(one word)
Sample: *Helpless.*

Why do you think that is? What's the backstory? ____________________
Sample: *Personal loss.*

When I see, touch, or connect to this charm, I perceive this threat to my well-being ____.
Sample: *Repetition of loss and an experience of grief and suffering. Rejection or abandonment.*

Is there an ingrained script? When confronted with this perceived threat, I tell myself this story: ____

____

Sample: *Catastrophizing. I always assume the worst. The impermanence of happiness, so why bother?*

Action is the antidote to anxiety: I can and will do this for my Highest Good:

____

____

Sample: *Romanticize life. Find positive ways to change neural pathways. Deepen connection to Spirit. Stop burying feelings.*

I can rely on these skills, resources, or strengths: ____________________
Sample: *Creativity. Resilience. Humor. Work that supports that consciousness survives death.*

I harness my fear and transmute it into valuable insight. I'm grateful for this key step in my journey for self-awareness. What personal wisdom has this charm given me?____

Sample: *The presence of unprocessed grief. The importance of surrender and acceptance.*

Make some notes. When casting for others, what new descriptive words, meanings, insight, or appreciation can you apply to this charm?

Sample: *Explore the symbol not only as an ending, but as a representation of fears, avoidance, or the interment of painful truths. How might the coffin be conveying the best way to live life on life's terms?*

After having completed this exercise for a few different charms, look back at your highlighted words. Are there any repetitions or similarities? If so, is there a theme emerging? Please note that if you ever feel like there's no work in the world that will help you bond with an individual piece, or the timing, for one deeply personal reason or another, just isn't right, remove it from your kit. Replace it. Reframe the meaning. Make changes that support a positive and happy headspace.

> *We don't see things as they are,*
> *we see them as we are.*
> —Anaïs Nin

Projection: I Know You Are But What Am I?

There's a good chance that we all do this once every day—sometimes twice. In most cases, it's a completely normal human thing to do. We take our own crap and baggage, negative and positive—thoughts, beliefs, emotions, actions, impulses, desires, ideals, or standards—and attribute or project them onto someone or something else. It's largely unconscious, and we're blissfully unaware that we're even doing it. Sometimes, the experts say, it's a defense mechanism that's protecting us from recognizing or taking personal accountability for things we need to work on. This could come from a place of insecurity, fear, lack of self-esteem, or inner conflict; it's the inner rift that keeps on giving. One classic textbook example of projection is the unfaithful partner who wrongly accuses their significant other of having an affair. It's not me—*never me*—it's you—*always you*. If you find yourself being overly critical (or flattering) of another person for apparently no good reason, ask where that annoying (or absolutely fabulous) characteristic might inhabit you. For instance, I can't, in all good conscience, berate my partner for having way too much stuff when there are five new tarot decks waiting for me in the mailbox. Not to mention that new mug because the others don't have a mushroom handle.

As far as I know, there isn't a framed psychology degree hanging on my wall (just a velvet painting of dogs playing poker). But as a diviner, I strive to become more aware of personal triggers and my own mythic themes and nonsense. When reading for others, in order to maintain peak objectivity and awareness it's always good to know where you end and your sitter begins. If you start projecting your pet problems onto a sitter's unfolding narrative, you run the risk of hijacking the reading. It becomes all about you, in which case, the divination either won't resonate with your sitter or, worse, they'll internalize misguided messages and leave your table less empowered and more vulnerable than when they arrived.

Charms are a powerful symbolic tool that can open dialogues with the unconscious in a playful and nonthreatening way. Here's how your charms can help you develop more self-awareness.

Pick a charm. *(Fleur-de-Lis—**reversed**)*

What does the charm mean to you: *(merit, honor, medal, award, recognition—**reversed**)*

Inhabit the charm. You are the charm. Complete this sentence: I am ________________. *(Unrecognized: I'm not honoring my accomplishments.)*

How might this make sense as a personal belief, impulse, or issue? *(I have issues being in the spotlight and accepting praise.)*

How might this be expressed as a projection onto someone or something? *(OMG! That person is so vain, egotistical, and unconscionable in the way they shamelessly promote themselves.)*

How can you accept, love, and heal that part of you and learn to walk a mile in someone else's shoes? *(By giving myself permission to be proud of my own accomplishments, learning the difference between humility and lack of self-esteem, choosing to be humble, but also acknowledging that this isn't everyone else's path and respecting that they may be working through their own issues.)*

Tip: If you've pulled a reversed charm, before you put it back into its tin or bowl, turn it around and rescript your first-person description in the positive. (I am honored, praised, and recognized.)

Projection can be a pretty common dynamic in a love, romance, and relationships reading. Which one of your charms would best represent this self-protective coping mechanism? A movie projector?

Interpretation

HELP! WHAT DOES IT ALL MEAN?

Blessed, Stressed, and Charm-Obsessed (Your Next T-shirt)

Quick review. You've curated at least one kit of kitschy charms. You've housed, pampered, then energized them with meaning and awe. You know how to keep them off the floor. You've found your preferred casting surface(s). Your toss, flick, or sprinkling technique supports your method. Now the real initiation, the labor of love begins: the analysis. You get to make sense of a random scattering of seemingly nonsensical items. Yay!

I won't lie. Learning how to navigate larger, more sprawling castings can at times be maddening and bewildering. It will call you out of your comfort zone. It will push you beyond what you thought you knew and challenge you to expand your awareness. You might briefly survey the casting with mortal instincts and try to tackle it all at once. If I had a wooden nickel for every time that I felt queasy at the enormity of it all, I could build an ark. My head spins: *Where do I start? There's too many of you! What's this one mean again? Why are you reversed, upside down, and at the bottom of a pile? How did you get in my candle?*

And then . . .

You'll breathe, pick up your pointer, and get ready to rock the reading one section at a time. Soon you'll be interpreting the whole shebang, turning tiny base materials into conduits of golden wisdom. There's nothing like it. Equipped with an open mind and heart, a shift in consciousness, and a few key basics, you'll stay on the front foot and never look back.

Don't Just Want It—Will It.

Before we get knee-deep in the hoopla, let's spitball some points of view.

Charm casting is a highly individual process. There's no right way: just your way. You or your sitter will understand every charm differently based on a personal filter of life experience and higher consciousness or subconscious recognition. If your innate method of casting and interpretation is giving you results and validation, honor it. Always trust your own intuition over more popular or traditional charm meanings—every time. That said, should something new *ever* spark your imagination, don't stand on ceremony. Take it for a test spin. No harm, no foul.

If you find that after a cast, you've formed a habit of discounting, removing, or altering the position of pieces, be kind but maybe ask yourself why. And be honest with yourself. If it's because you've let the universe know that *this is how I roll*, survey says, *Good answer.* Carry on. Let it be known that any item that dares fall at the bottom of a pile, reversed, or out of bounds—or that makes not one lick of sense (in that precise moment) will be disregarded. If, however, it's because you're unsure of how to deal with these unruly pieces, that's about to change. All of these charms, convenient to read or not, have presented for a reason. Had they not, they'd still be in the box or bowl with the others waiting for their close-up.

Are you ever overwhelmed by too many pieces for a short reading? Do any feel extraneous, like they're just muddying the clarity of the message? If so, maybe try throwing fewer. Do you aesthetically dislike the look or lack of detail of reversed charms? If possible, you can swap those charms out over time for 3D versions. Are you getting a lot of rowdy runaways and unmanageable mounds? Maybe revisit and tweak your casting technique. It takes time and practice, but you'll get it just the way you like it. And if you still get these unhappy landings the odd time, no biggie—you'll learn how to read these castings as well.

Remember what I said about getting your fingers into a casting? *Land sakes, where are my smelling salts?* Well, never mind—for the moment at least. There's a more hands-on method where a few randomly selected pieces get thrown onto a surface. You would then connect with the pieces by touching them and moving them around. Intuitively, it might feel like one just wants to sit with another or charms with like energies and meanings are slid together to reinforce a theme. Not only will this method yield swift and shiny nuggets of insight for a daily, general draw, but it's a great way to bond with your charms. You'll get to lavish singular focus on individual pieces and note how they play with others. They can also be cast beside or over symbol-rich tarot or oracle cards for a more layered reading.

The Charm Café: An Exercise

Lay out a random fingerful of charms in front of you. (This isn't a divination, so it's perfectly reasonable that you'll get an odd, *unattuned* assortment, which makes this more challenging.) Are there any kindred pieces in this grouping? In what way are these pieces similar? What traits do they share? What makes them unique? Do you need to revisit any meanings?

Study pairs of charms. Pick two and push them together. Imagine that they are strangers who meet at a café. How would they introduce themselves to one another?

Hello, I'm ______________________, and I act, think, behave, or express in this manner: ______________________________________.

Will they get along? Why? If they're not kindred, might they disagree or argue? Over what? What might one think about the other? How could one potentially help or hinder the other? When these two individual voices combine, how do they merge to create a third meaning: the sum of the two parts? When you're done, change up the pairings, then study the new and always entertaining dialogue. We'll get to an example of this shortly. Stay tuned...

Scribble

You can find small wooden live-edge discs at a local dollar store for peanuts. Or make them (if you don't associate sawing wood with losing limbs). They make a great mini stage or chairs for your Charm Café. I've propped one up on a small mason jar. Seat your pieces in the center, then eavesdrop on their conversation.

Popping the Question

Fact: Questions matter. Equally important to the art of mining insightful answers is the way you craft your questions. When the Wee Ones are strewn about, doing what they do best—casting you adrift in a storm surge of answers—the *artful ask* keeps you anchored to your context. Said notoriously brainy Albert Einstein, "If I had an hour to solve a problem and my life depended on the solution, I would spend the first fifty-five minutes determining the proper question to ask, for once I know the proper question, I could solve the problem in less than five minutes."

The diviner's question, moreover, isn't just a function of curiosity; it's also a petition to Spirit. Let's, for a moment, personify the universe. There it sits in a throne—or a rocking recliner (you decide)—thumbing through a penny dreadful, and the hotline rings. The universe is an active listener, and given a half-baked, hazy, unfocused, or convoluted question, there won't be any congenial attempts to figure out exactly what's meant. It preternaturally presumes that the question is perfect. And so, too, will be the corresponding result. When working with charms, which are multifaceted symbols, if you don't give them an informed platform upon which to express, you'll also get the smallest piece of them. And the interpretation process will feel like dragging a comb through tangled hair.

Close-Ended vs. Open-Ended Questions

A journalist is given a high-profile assignment. They've been flown to Schenectady to interview the hottest new chef. Chef's busy and cranky. For a change, he's agreed to answer one question.

Journo: *Chef, is it true your restaurant serves caviar with a mother-of-pearl spoon?*

Chef: *Yes.*

And . . . game over. *Thanks for coming out.* There's a time and place for quick and dirty *yes or no* work. Clearly, this wasn't it. This is an example of a closed-ended question. Go fishing without proper tackle and you'll catch a rubber boot. Instead, rework your queries so that they're open-ended. In other words, they can't be answered with a limited yes or no reply. The right open-ended question will yield a windfall of topic-specific information. If asked, *Chef, why does your restaurant serve caviar with a mother-of-pearl spoon? What do we need to know about spoons and caviar? Can you elaborate?* He'll open up and explain that metal spoons will oxidize the caviar and ruin the taste, which is infinitely more obliging than *yes.*

The Fully Loaded Question

What's this? You know, that rhetorical ask that already assumes or is imbued with a heavy bias regarding the answer. If a reader's convinced that someone's cheating and throws charms as an afterthought—what's the point? They'll just head into the reading searching for charms that support and validate their hypothesis, shoving square pegs into round holes. Avoid this trap.

Once you've crafted your *artful* question, go into your readings neutral, detached, receptive, but completely impartial. You'll increase your accuracy and build solid charm casting muscles by expecting the unexpected.

Context vs. Subtext: The Inside Story

Context is a subject, a topic. It's a frame of reference. It stares you right in the face. Subtext, on the other hand, is when there's more than meets the eye. It's what lies beneath and between the lines. It's what's meant, but not what's actually been said, the inside story. When you're working with symbols, there'll be astounding examples of subtext. If you learn how to spot them, your readings will take on a whole new and more specific dimension of meaning.

If our context is health and well-being, let's examine this combination: a pink-glazed **doughnut** charm (sweet treat, indulgence, decadence) lands on a *cutesy* plastic **teddy bear**. It has a see-through body which is filled with sparkles. We know bears love honey. Are these two charms saying pamper yourself with something sweet? That's one quick surface interpretation, but keep digging. Can you pick up the subtext? What might these two charms be articulating about a deeper issue?

Let's parse it out: Bear with *honey* (sugar doughnut). This makes it **happy** and **full**. Remember, we can see the contents of this particular charm's body, its belly and head, and it's already full of big sparkles. So we can deduce that the **ingestion** of sweet things is probably not a one-off. It could very well be a **habit**. In this manner, these two charms combine to reveal a subtext of *overindulgence*. Now you would look around and read to determine where, how, and why this overindulgence is being experienced. How is it affecting the sitter's health or well-being? Who knows? It could be something other than sugar that's dispensing the dopamine or filling the emptiness (also suggested by the hole in the doughnut). It could be related to work, a relationship, shopping, or even the need to habitually solve other people's problems.

Scribble

During a casting, should your inner voice say, "Ask your sitter," trust it. Your sitter always holds the answers. I'd pulled a few charms for a client. She had just begun a new life and career-changing field of study. I randomly pulled another charm—one of my hands, palm down, which to me means taking. This didn't resonate. Ask your sitter. "So what does this mean to you?" I searched, and she began laughing. She was studying massage therapy.

Theme Catcher

A theme, as we learned in Miss Abernathy's English class, is the *driving* idea or concept behind a story. *Romeo and Juliet* is a play about young (nauseating) love, but one of the underlying themes is about duty and the legacy of an old family conflict. The more you cast, the more you'll discover that your casting surface is a perfect theme catcher. Pay attention to emerging themes because they're often linked to important lessons, initiations, or transitions. A good way to tell if you've snagged a theme is by a random repetition of like-minded charms. They don't need to be close to each other or in the same grouping. Say a coffin lands in the seer's bull's-eye. You might read this, first and foremost, as an ending with considerable impact, yet if the rest of your casting surface is swimming with an octopus, crab, shovel, or fish, you may want to explore an additional layer—an underlying theme of deeply buried emotional issues.

Divination vs. Free Association

In a divination, you're mostly working with your charm's assigned meanings. Once the charms are cast, you become the mystic master of ceremonies and intuit an interpretation for your sitter. There's also another way of putting the Wee Ones into service. This method favors a more therapeutic approach and involves an interactive technique called free association. In these sessions, your charms are used to open dialogues with both the conscious and the unconscious. They'll be used as symbols that want to inspire spontaneous expression—whatever springs to mind: words, a thought, memory, feeling, or experience.

Instead of being the interpreter of a charm, when using this free association technique, you become the keeper of a safe and supportive space within which your sitter can read their own charms. You'll ask your sitter, off the top of their head, to tell you what a randomly selected piece means to them. How do *they* understand that piece? If you're casting a charm over an illustrated tarot or oracle card, ask them to also describe where the charm's landed. How do they align with that symbol, detail or area? File away the meaning of the card for the moment, and instead encourage a stream-of-consciousness exploration of the richly layered allegory.

You'll also be guided to ask artful leading or follow-up questions. This shared way of working with charms can help your sitters make their own key connections, which only deepens their understanding of self and situation—and strengthens the resonance and healing potential of their aha moments. How do you know a sitter's had an aha moment? Their whole face, energy and body language transform.

Divination and Free Association: DIY Grimoire Casting Chart

Casting charms over a DIY chart—a page filled with your own written words—combines the best of both metaphysical and psychological worlds.

Using a plastic template, ruler, or thin washi tape, create a grid, either a square of nine or sixteen that can be stored in your casting grimoire. Decide if you want a general or situation-specific oracle, which is ideal if you want to keep checking the pulse of an ongoing issue. Or you can fill these squares with prompts that have been divined using stichomancy.

Pull out a favorite book. Open it randomly to a page. Close your eyes. Let your index finger locate a word. Write it down. Repeat until you have enough words to fill the squares of your grid. By the way, it's OK to cheat and swap out words like *gorgonzola* for something more serviceable, like *mastery*. Did these randomly selected words come together to form a context for the chart? Is there a theme?

When your chart is completed, you can randomly pick pieces and position them in every square. Or cast only a few charms and free-associate their meanings. Should a charm fall on a line between squares, don't write it off or

blend the meaning of both squares. Why? Let's think about that for a minute. Logistically, your piece had no way of landing between this square and one of the many that it wasn't touching.

Alternatively, you gorgeous, gifted diviner, try this: Take a mental snapshot of the charm and the two squares. Close your eyes. Try and feel—or see in your mind's eye—a pull to one side (square) or the other. Is this pull strong? If so, connect your charm with that charged square and interpret a message. Or is it possibly stuck? If you can't feel a definitive pull to one side or the other, forget the context of the squares and free-associate with the charm itself. In any case, if your piece didn't fall more or less clearly in the middle of a square, you might want to explore the idea of resistance, hesitance, avoidance, and a need for more reflection on the meaning and message of that charm.

Tiny, Shiny Psychic Therapy

There's no denying that a bowl full of tiny, shiny things looks like a treasure chest or toy box. Unlike wildly misunderstood tarot cards, this divinatory tool won't, at a glance, threaten or shut down a sitter. When they see your charms, their eyes widen with wonder, and they'll want to run their hands through them and play. Charms appeal to that inner child who still has memories, feelings, and possibly unfulfilled needs associated with their past that may still be influencing their present and potential.

The Mission Possible Statement: If you or a sitter need clarity and actionable steps toward working through, better understanding, or resolving an issue, try this little exercise. Rummage through the charms. Take your time. Preselect two to four pieces that best convey the story and situation. What happened? Lay them out in front of you. One by one, hold the piece and describe why you chose it. What does each piece represent? Now, ask what some therapists call the miracle question: *What would life look like if you could just take your pointer and zap away the problem?* Preselect two to four more charms that best symbolize what your life could be like following a solution-based change. Let these pieces describe what would be different. How *would* you feel? Who *would* you be? What *could* you do? What *might* you have? Again, review each one and connect with why you chose these specific pieces.

Now randomly select one to three new castmates and just add them to the others. Mix up all of the pieces in front of you. Without thinking about it, arrange them in a horizontal line that just feels right. Get a pen and paper. Assign a quick meaning, word or brief phrase to each charm, and begin cobbling these words together into a crude, stream-of-consciousness sentence. It doesn't have to be pretty or make sense. Once that's done, identify one or a few pieces with movement or distinct directionality, like leaping dolphins, a train, or rising star. Do these pieces feel like they're about to tell you to do something? If so, move them to the front of the line. At this stage, the rest of your charms may start "walking"—feeling like they want to go somewhere else in the lineup. Should this happen, go ahead and from a completely intuitive place tweak the order—now's the time. Here your charms are stepping into service to help you access a solution or strategy, as well as renew confidence and control. Given that you now have a new order, as well as the addition of randomly divined charms, if, wondrously, fresh or different meanings or even odd words or phrases present, honor them. Don't be taken aback if you wonder, *Who is this? This doesn't sound like me at all.* Evidently, Charmspeak and Spirit are similar dialects.

Pause for a beat. Then, charm-by-charm, begin (automatic) rewriting, channeling and polishing your message into a mission-possible statement: I (do this) ____________________ BY OR USING (these gifts and resources) ____________________ IN ORDER TO (be, think, have, create, feel, allow, enjoy, receive, release, achieve, shift, celebrate, etc.) ____________________.

Instant vs. Latent Gut Hits

I was taught that when interpreting a charm, go with your immediate gut hit: to trust that download because it sidesteps the path and peril of too much logical thought, which, as you know, kills the vibe of a good divination. But as someone who has trouble leaving the comfortable chaos of my head, I could not—and I still cannot. And so I offer you this quick aside. If gut hits are ready, willing, and available, go with these first impressions and instincts. This is your style. It's the popular method, and clearly, it's working for you. If, however, things aren't sparking immediately, don't you dare worry or doubt yourself—instead, walk away. Leave your casting intact and hold space for that message. Do something dull and mindless. Fold laundry; starch your casting cloths (heh heh); clean out your closet. While your mind is in limbo elsewhere, the message *will* arrive. It's late to the party, maybe, but it arrives in style. This is the swagger of the latent hit.

Interpretation vs. Synthesis

What's the diff? When we're interpreting a charm, we're translating its meaning, plain and simple. The badminton birdie is racket-sport equipment. It's something that goes back and forth. The top left-hand quadrant of the casting surface represents past influences. Think of a granny square quilt. Interpretation is like the crafty completion of one small part of a larger project. Synthesis, however, is the masterful process of weaving together all of your scraps of information into a message that fully covers the context—from top to tail.

It's during this advanced stage of the reading that you'll gain profound insight into a potential theme, patterns, timing, multiple storylines, influences, and predicted outcomes. It's good to be a great charm caster; it's great to be a good synthesizer.

Attuning and Validating Charms

Have you ever had this experience with any of your sacred tools? You're ready to rumble but their vital signs are absent—they are unresponsive. Baffled and blocked, you're sitting in front of an indecipherable mess o' nothin'. Or they're responding in a tone for which you have zero tolerance: hissing and spewing out the most negative, hateful, and fear-provoking sides of themselves. In both cases, you just know something's off big-time.

Should this happen, you may need to do an honest self-check first. How are you? Are you feeling stressed, under the weather, or ungrounded? If so, it's OK. We've all been there. Your tool could be reacting to some energetic dissonance. Give yourself and your tool some space. Wrap it up; tomorrow's a new day. Or take a brief walk and return to work when you're cruising at a better altitude. If you know your spirits are high, then by process of elimination—yes, it's your tool. Assuming it's not like Annabelle (get thee to the Warren Museum), your tool might just need an energetic adjustment.

Should your charms ever feel like strangers, dull and heavy, send them to the charm spa (page 58) because when you and your charms are perfectly *attuned*—energetically sympatico—they'll purr and perform for you—as if you're stepping on the accelerator of a Ferrari. What thrust! Such response! They'll offer up pieces that just click into place—and often honor your question by giving you a saucy wink—the **validating charm**. If you're asking about travel, you'll randomly pull an airplane or a suitcase. If you're wondering what to know about that corporate interview, behold the necktie. Validating charms in and of themselves aren't the answer, but their special function is to let you know, as the caster, that you're on the right path. You're in a state of grace.

Storytime: I wanted to buy an old, used trailer to park in our driveway and have as a reading room and office. I asked the charms, *What could I expect from this fabulous inspiration?* I expected the expected: the glowing *awesome* and *best-idea-ever* charms. Instead, I pulled the knife, scissors, cleaver, train, ax, and devil. I careened into denial. Were these charms *mildly* hinting that the trailer could be a *train wreck of an idea?*—Nah! I drew again. All negative. Appallingly so. Then I booked a reading with a highly respected tarot reader and asked her the same question. Surely, blessed with much keener insight and angelic kindness, she would straighten out this mess. Her answer? *NO. Absolutely and unequivocally, don't do this idiotic, imbecilic thing.* So we bought the trailer. A weasel of a neighbor called the dedicated officers at the town, and we had to sell it within a very short span of time. Moral of this story? When you're confident that your charms are properly attuned, you have two choices: 1) honor them and trust your intuitive and psychic gifts or 2) pay for a professional to tell you the exact same thing. Good talk.

The Calm before the Casting: A Pep Talk

- Know your charms. They're an extension of you.
- Know the anatomy of your casting surface; it's an extension of your context.
- Begin with a clear, well-thought-out question. If you lose your way through your casting, revisit it to get back on track.
- A casting is like a snapshot: You can glean a high probability of an outcome based on a predisposition to make certain choices; but no result is etched in stone. The future is subject to free will. Look to see if the charms are trying to open a dialogue about those choices.

Out of Hand: Now We Dance

Truth: I can't really teach you how to interpret and synthesize a casting. That's because no two castings will ever be alike and no two souls will ever have carbon copy filters for incoming information (or the same guides). Together, however, we'll promenade through a picturesque charmscape, and I can point out some of the main attractions. In no time at all, you'll have your own escapades to look forward to, and with pluck and perseverance, you'll emerge from the labyrinth a living legend, wearing a laurel wreath, quivering with pride and *trinketfreude.*

> *Trinketfreude:* deriving enormous pleasure from humanizing small inanimate objects. It's a thing.

The Inner Circle

For instructional purposes, I'll be sharing a method of casting into a circle because it covers all of the basics. If you're new to charm casting, working without the convenience of an illustrated surface can feel like riding your first bike without training wheels. Still, learning this method will strengthen your foundational skills, which can then be applied with ease and élan to any other format.

While this method of casting starts and then radiates outward from the center, it's interpreted and synthesized *as a whole.* It gives your charms leeway—not *just or always* the surface areas—to guide you through time and space by beginning and blowing out narratives in all of the extraordinary ways that they do. That said, your point of reference at any given moment will still largely rely on intentions that you've set for the casting surface and look-at-me pieces. You'll get used to working in seemingly unrelated sections with cryptic chunks of information and meaning, until gradually the casting gains momentum—and it all comes together.

Every charmscape will be different and present its own agenda and timing. I just trust that my charms, simply in the way they land and combine, will have their own attuned means of letting me know what was, is, and will more than likely be. We know that the past is a mental construct that no longer exists, but there could be a situation or a story with its roots in the past, its tendrils in the present, and its sights firmly fixed on affecting the future, auspiciously or inauspiciously. All of this can be conveyed in a few different ways. Maybe you too will have a "past" or "old" VIP piece. If it lands with a car, this isn't a new car; if the charm is reversed and the grouping includes something medical, maybe the charms are bringing up a present or future treatment of an old injury sustained in an accident. Sometimes the origin of a story can be found in or around the center, and then it blows out from there. Study your patterns. In a line, time always passes from left to right. Some lines of charms want to be read narratively: this happens, then that, then this, until that, but then—finally—this. The end. Thanks for coming out.

Depending on the quantity of charms in your castings, of course, expect to be dealing with patterns, combinations, clusters and pileups, and direct and indirect communication between the pieces that span more than one house and numerological path. Do you have to blend charm and surface area meanings every time? That's entirely your call. Ask the pattern: *What's the buzz? Where are you directing me?* Follow the breadcrumbs and see where they lead. I typically blend in the meanings for houses and numbered paths—but not always and maybe not for every charm or pattern. I might just do this for the ones that clearly land in a segment or on a path or, on revisitation to an area, when pieces are driving me to keep investigating. I'll get a strong sense that something's still missing and waiting for me to make the connection. It depends on the reading. How will you know? You just will.

It's safe to say that whenever a single charm clearly lands in a specific quadrant, segment (house), or path, blend in that extra information. Looks like that book charm in the ninth house of Sagittarius gets published. How will you interpret any charm that touches one of your impact beads? While it's far from the center, even as an indirect influence, it's fully charged and loaded with the meaning of that numbered path. On occasion, you'll get that charm that ends a line. And it sits separately, a beat away from the others, in its own kingdom, like it's an epilogue or an exclamation mark at the end of a sentence. Damn straight, I'm rushing to explore that area's meaning. Over time you'll master an awareness of how to best deploy your instincts and intuition. And these will be challenged differently with every charmscape. Truly, this is why casting never gets tired.

Let's get down to the gritty details of the countless crazy ways that charms like to express. These are some of the main elements and building blocks of technique, the *artful* consideration of which will consistently support many layered, nuanced, and deeply insightful interpretations.

> *Artful:* An art combined with a little ancient nose twitchery and moting into being.

Dispersion and Distance

Before you begin reading, take a peek at the distribution of your charms. Is everything clumped together in one area of your surface? Unless you're Sir Edmund Hillary, there's no point scaling this mass. Two things can help: 1) revisiting page 96 on throwing technique and 2) dynamite. Furthermore, are there lots of charms outside of your circle or who knows where? Also not ideal. In either of these extremes, consider recasting for a happier and more sensible landing.

While first scanning the charmscape, note factors such as flow, space, traffic, physical patterns, balance or imbalance, movement, blockages, repetition or duplication of similar charms, loners, jumpers, validating charms. Speak to your cast and crew. Say, *Here I am, my darlings, who wants a piece of me?* Anticipate a chorus of whispers and too much raw feedback too soon. But hold on to it. Those first impressions and sparks of insight begin to ignite the process of analysis.

Consider distance. Fact: The closer a charm is to anything—a look-at-me piece (another charm, VIP, word chain, base kit bracelet, impact bead) or area (center, perimeter)—the greater the significance and impact of that influence.

There will also be times when your pieces fall far away from one another. They stand their own ground, and in doing so, pull focus in their own quiet way. Distance or a *missed chance at interconnection* with another kindred castmate should always pique curiosity. Say, for instance, you have a **nest** charm in combination with an **institution** in one area. You now notice a kindred, companion, or similarly themed castmate—a **bird**—perched elsewhere. It's on path 1 (the self, solitary, new beginnings), and its beak is pointing away from the nest and outside of the circle. Given these factors—the grouping (a nest and an official building), distance, and directionality of the bird—it's reasonable to suppose that your sitter's going through empty-nest syndrome. The **bird** is clearly focusing elsewhere. Has it flown the coop to attend university or college? Check to see if anything's happening in the ninth house of education and higher learning. At this early stage of the game, I wouldn't rule out jail. If that nest and institution charm have landed in the twelfth house, orange might be the new tweed.

You'll get into the habit of approaching every quirk with a question and a wry furrowing of the brow. On cursory inspection, faraway and runaway pieces seem antisocial, like they aren't *directly* chatting, being influenced, or wanting to play the same game with their castmates. You could be right. This kind of casting can even feel naked and sparse. So do you throw a few more charms in to beef it up and fill in the gaps? You could. It's also possible that this casting isn't firing on a lot of different levels. It might be trying to drive home a few no-frills but vital kinds of points. Done and done. Yet sometimes loners could still be communicating indirectly, and the way they do this will be explained when we look at their physical characteristics and directionality.

Look-at-Me Areas and Pieces

Start here: What's landed, if anything, inside, on, or around the seer's bull's-eye? Read this first. Whatever falls into the bracelet is like a keynote speaker: it presents on behalf of the significator and sets the agenda for the casting.

Validating charms that fall into the center (*wha-whaaat?*) augment the importance of the question, and the reading—of everything, really. It's like the seer's eye is wide-open and just winked at you. As a rule, charms that present in or closest to the center take precedence. They need your focus first. Deal with the pieces that have landed farther away after you're clear on what's happening in or around the middle.

Continue here: Next note and read the pieces that are outside of the bracelet but touching or near the edge. These *downtown* pieces might be flying solo or in a formation with other castmates as part of a combination, cluster, or line. In this case, they'll be teaming up to bring in breaking news, the dish and dirt, key details, a thickening plot, or a backstory that still packs a wallop—whatever is on the tip of those trinket tongues, you can expect it to be an integral part of the main narrative. If a charm is laying on top of the seer's eye, connect energetically and decide if it's trying to get in . . . or crawl out.

Charms that have settled in the outskirts or *suburbs* of your circle could be contributing incidental details, with a milder or more indirect influence. They're still important to the story, but have a more *oh-and-another-thing* or *by-the-way* kind of tone. They could even be weaving additional, unrelated, or parallel storylines. You won't know for sure unless you're grounded in the central idea of the reading.

If the center is empty, you'll need to finish the reading and then form an understanding of why nothing required heightened attention. In some instances, it could be because an issue has been downgraded and the casting is taking you through the remnants or fallout. Or your sitter, on some level, might be putting up some conscious or unconscious resistance to any highest-good guidance. Maybe they're not ready to face or push through what they really don't want to do. If these blockages are in place, be gentle. No matter what, you've planted a seed and shown your sitter the watering can.

Preselected significators, VIPs, word chains *go next.* If you're using any preselected charms or specialty kit pieces, locate and feel these out first. They'll represent the main pillars of the reading, the principal players (you and other significators that are relevant to the narrative), life areas (love, finance, family, etc.), or a hot topic (real estate deal, retirement, a business, trade school vs. university vs. jail, etc.). Let your eyeballs wander through the charmscape. What base kit charms have presented with these pieces and how are they showing up? Note where and how they've all landed; peruse the groupings and see if you can make any cursory connections. What look-at-me pieces/patterns have landed closest to the center? Which ones are closest to one another? Is there a clear path and flow between pieces/patterns? Or are there barriers that bring restrictions? *Rules, be damned, do you feel inexplicably drawn anywhere first?*

Did any of these key pieces/patterns land in a house or on a path? If so, work with that layer of meaning. (For example, your significator piece, either alone or part of a pattern, has landed in the first house of Aries. This reading is—cue the fanfare—*all about you.*) If a piece is part of a pattern that sprawls past a few set house or path boundaries, don't fret. Feel it out. Make a choice to use or disregard area meanings—*for the moment*—while you're getting a handle on the charmspeak. If, later on, you sense a need for additional details, you can, emotional support pointer in hand, always backtrack to that grouping when it's not so overwhelming.

The Outcasts: Jumpers and Out-of-Play Pieces, Loners, Reversals, and Other Oddballs

You'll have to make up your mind as to how you're going to read the outcasts that don't land picture perfect. You'll have the option, of course, of showing them who's boss by turning them over and around or giving them the cold shoulder or the boot. But that's not very nice. They went out of their way to be difficult, so it pays to find out why. Here's a few alternative suggestions to mull over. See if they work for you.

Jumpers: There are two kinds. First, there's the naughty leap. Your charm lands outside of the casting circle, but it's still close enough for you to hear its tale and feel its emotion. Then, there's the X-treme jumper. Either it has stage fright—or it's an asshole. Whatever the reasoning, it had better things to do than work with you or the team. If you can find it, pick it up. Briefly interpret it. Ask why that cake didn't make it to the wedding. Or why that sunflower bent toward the shade. Place it on the table next to your casting. Once you've finished your reading, have some fun. Close your eyes and throw it back into the casting. How did it land? Reinterpret that section and see how its presence could have made a difference. Does something new reveal itself to you?

In or out of play? A typical classification for charms falling outside of a designated surface is *out of play*. And so they're discarded or disregarded. Instead, why not keep them *in play*? These pieces are, after all, full of beans and running riot. They're defiant, mavericks. They've bolted out of bounds and can be read as something that's *out of control*. Depending on the positioning and directionality of the charm, it could also be trying to claw its way back onto the casting surface. Why not? Stranger things have happened. Evidently, it still seeks attention, but it's the charm that asks, *Can I talk to you in private*?

Check two things: 1) What, if anything, sits between this rogue charm and the center of the casting. How might this connect to the jumper, like what did it run from? 2) Using your charmala and set intentions as a guide, outside of which quadrant, house, or numbered path has it landed? Use this as an opportunity to gain insight into an out-of-control situation or life area that wants more discipline, love, work, or conscious awareness.

Loners: These are in-play charms that are still outliers. They're alone in fortune's crowd. They carry simple, *that's-the-facts-Jack* messages. For good measure, pay attention to a loner's precise location and its area meaning. Check its proximity to the center (primary impact) or outer edge of the circle (secondary). Review what's close. Sometimes loners seem like they should have been part of a grouping. It makes me wonder, *Why isn't it with those peeps? What's that all about?* Nothing maybe—but it pays to snoop, because there's often heady stuff in the shadows.

We'll delve into this again (see the section on directionality on page 144), but observe a single charm's physical characteristics and presentation. Does it have a pronounced feature that's trying to direct your focus somewhere else on the casting surface? Look for an *indirect* communication between your loners and other pieces. *What are they whispering to one another*? Are they getting along, nodding in accord? Are they like-minded or themed charms with a similar energy? Or is there a thinly veiled threat, like a sharp skate blade being brandished at a balloon? Does it seem like one is gossiping or talking absolute rubbish behind the other's back? Even if this were true, don't be shocked. Remember that the Wee Ones are all upstanding and good; some might just be cast into the role of villain to make a point.

Reversals and other oddballs: When a 2D charm lands face (and detailed side) down, you may have to flip it over so you can see what it is. Three-dimensional charms also have backs, but they're not only easier to deal with, they often have more to work with. Then you'll need to decide whether to read or not to read. That is the question. I say, go for it. Reversals are cloaked, like a secret society with their own muted mannerisms and codes. They're not speaking in their loudest and fullest voice. Their sotto voce is a dramatic reduction in volume in order to secure your heightened attention. Sometimes, they're hiding something—their face or true nature. Or they're presenting a shadow, inauspicious energy, or the opposite of their core meaning.

Should a hand vanity mirror land right side up, it's asking for self-reflection. Take a good, hard look in the mirror. When it's reversed, it's like, *Psssst, hey you. Yeah you. What aren't you ready to see?* When a car presents with all four tires in the air, it's a warning: the shiny side's down and the greasy side's up. *What needs more attention to safety?* Two brightly colored flower charms in your casting present petal side down. So ephemeral, these beautiful blooms have withered and fallen away. Perhaps there's a theme emerging of a need to take and make time *to smell the roses.*

Friendly heads-up: Charms love a bit of drama to keep us engaged. They'll show up all cattywampus, not only reversed but upside down, leaning this way or that, standing upright, on their heads, or intimately tangled in another piece. Work with their physicality. The vertical (sinking) battleship lands in combination with an overturned lounge chair. Too funny! Your stand-up comedy charms have just remarked that something's as useful as rearranging the deck chairs on the *Titanic*.

Watch . . . them . . . all. Closely.

Characteristics and directionality: This much we know: Each piece is different, distinguished by its physical attributes of color, texture, composition, curves, points, blades, bowls, holes, edges, corners, stems, hooks, and body parts, for example. These features give your piece its unique character, body language, and takeaway, an emotional and energetic impression that supports the interpretation.

This we learn: Our charms are inanimate—until they hit the casting surface. Then they can swim, gallop, run, fly, ski, sauté, conjure spirits, sit in chairs, go fishing, and roll dung balls, for starters. And we get to work with this audacious behavior. If a charm has a head with eyes or an elongated feature like an arm, it can stare or point. *Where are they redirecting your focus?* Follow that sightline. Even if it's inverted, like a hanged man—*what's it looking at?* If your piece implies motion, like a car, animal, bus, or ship, *where's it going?* Tag along. Is it a hammer, knife, or gavel? *Is it ready to strike or is it at rest?* A plane or a butterfly? *Is it taking off or landing?* Where's the horse pulling its cart? Is a dagger threatening, severing, stabbing, or being pulled out of something valiantly like the sword in the stone? It never ceases to amaze me how a charm's characteristics can enable the most uncanny and intriguing interactions.

Either face up or reversed, some pieces are concave and become little bowls, like a bottle cap or thimble. A turtle nests in a reversed comedy and tragedy mask. *Until something's acknowledged, it's a slow process out of this drama.* Or they have cutout, peekaboo parts, like my visor charm or cage. This lets them seize, hug, swallow, cradle, protect, imprison, tempt, or trap their castmates. *What's caught in the spider's web?* Others, owing to sharp, bossy, aggressive, or tentacled bits, bite, strangle, sting, entangle, hook, crush, or threaten. It takes all kinds to form our castable community.

C'mon. Give it a go. Cast a soft glance over your reading. Hold your pointer over your circle and raise up those invisible paths to see if you can spot any covert connections between charms that are sitting apart from one another. They share confidences. They don't do this every time, but when they do chat indirectly, they're letting you into their dirty little secrets.

Scribble

Like Matryoshka dolls, pieces can nestle inside other larger charms and, unless you look, you won't know they're there until you're tucking the Wee Ones back into their tin. So really look. I completely missed seeing a jack stuck inside a badminton birdie. Good thing too. This coupling still stumps me to this day. What on earth do you think this combo meant?

Blockers, separators, ceilings, and dividers: Any charm that lands on top of another charm blocks or restrains the energy of that piece. Similarly, depending on where and how it lands—vertically, horizontally, or diagonally—a long or narrow piece such as a bar, nail, ladder, sewing needle, branch, saber, or bone can act as a barrier or boundary between pieces and storylines or signal a standoff. Like the old Checkpoint Charlie in a divided Berlin, it positions itself in a manner to dictate restrictions by cutting off the flow between pieces. You'll need to intuit your way through this rough country.

Certain pieces can also act like a bridge or a connector. Here's an example. A long sewing needle has a tapered point at one end and an eye at the other. Follow the point. Working with the motion of sewing and the needle's directionality, visualize the needle pulling and attaching any charm(s) sitting by the eye toward and to the charm(s) at the point. The needle itself imparts an atmosphere of labor or handiwork, so it will take some hands-on effort to fix, repair, or unite those two separate things.

The eyes don't have it: If necessary, keep a loupe, cheaters, or magnifiers on hand. Without magnification, you can miss a lot. I spied with my weary eyes a rider on a galloping horse, but hot diggity: it was actually a knight in plate armor, brandishing a tiny shield with a coat of arms. Love's truly in these details.

Castmates: Combinations, Groupings, and Pileups

WHEN TWO BECOME ONE: READING A COMBINATION: THE KERNEL AND THE HALO TECHNIQUE

Every charm has a *kernel*: the seed or nut, the most central part. This is the core meaning or simply its name—what you call it. It also has a *halo*. This is its radiant body, the atmosphere surrounding it—the feel and takeaway. This is the charm's spirit and energy.

Let's look at three boat charms—say a Viking longboat, a battleship, and a canoe. While they all share aspects of the same kernel because all are watercraft, they have completely different halos. When you're reading a combination of charms, get grounded in their respective kernels—then let their halos marry. This is where the magic happens. This is where you'll gain access to that synthesized meaning.

Remember that ol' Charm Café exercise? Using the charms in this bougie bistro scenario, here's an example of an oddball pairing—Cupid and battleship—and how these two strange bedfellows can merge and blend to create a third meaning. Let them introduce themselves to one another.

Cupid: I'm a hair-trigger matchmaker, an agent of passion and attraction, but hey, did you know that my dad Mars was the god of war, and my mom Venus, the goddess of love? Crazy, huh?

Battleship: Idiot. I'm a deadly serious WWII ship heading slowly and purposefully into battle.

Looking at this combination, a quick surface or kernel interpretation might be a love boat—but that doesn't feel right. The battleship is way too heavy energetically. Both of these charms share passion, the expression of which is mercurial in Cupid and purposeful in battleship. They both have the facet of war in common. When I soften my gaze and let their halos merge, I hear, *warmonger.* This is ideally, I believe, how Cupid's halo, its takeaway of passion and instigation, can best support the halo mission and aggressive mindset of the battleship.

Always honor your download. Revisit your question. Take a look at where the combination has landed, what it's next to, then let it find its *big-picture significance.* The charms could simply be telling you about a person who loves making mountains out of molehills or that instigates constant conflict because that's their jam.

Clusters and pileups: When charms fall in a cluster, begin by acknowledging them individually as separate ingredients, and then stir the pot (figuratively). You know you want to. What happens when a pumpkin, a tomato, and a racoon present in the same space? (No this isn't a joke. They haven't all walked into a bar with a priest and a parrot.) The masked racoon in this scenario, FYI, is staring at the pumpkin. There are a few ways that you can approach the interpretation of any grouping:

1. Literally. There's a racoon in your vegetable garden. They love fruits and vegetables.
2. Metaphorically. The simile compares two things by using *like* or *as. Gracious! This red dress makes me look like a ripe tomato.* When working with symbols, you'll be making a lot of metaphorical connections, because this figure of speech compares one thing to something else, and that something else is what sets off the light bulbs. *The harvested tomato and pumpkin = bounty, fruitfulness, abundance; Racoon = masked scavenger, thief, survivalism, opportunism, hidden agenda.* A possible synthesis might be a threat or fear that something or someone will try to scamper off with the *fruits of your diligent labor,* however that might resonate. It could be actual goods or even credit and accolades.

3. Idiomatically. You'll be reminded of a phrase or group of words: under the weather, beating around the bush, stairway to heaven.

4. Intuitively. Channeled through the filter of your own knowledge, observation, and free association, what arises? If the masked and hungry racoon had to gobble up one of these two items before getting caught, which would it be? What springs to mind? The red tomato is sweet and sun-ripened. It is *not* thick-skinned, like the pumpkin, and so it's easier to eat. The racoon, however, is still directing you to some good advice. It seems to say that you'll need to toughen up. Let an adversary know that you're not so easily vanquished.

5. Charm charades. This is rare, but it can happen. Sometimes your charms will get you to say a word. For instance, let's look at the guillotine. Typically, maybe, you'd associate it with cutting or severing. But, if you hear the word *execution*, for instance, go with it. And it could be the *execution* of a will or a task. Look for supporting evidence around that charm.

6. Always refer back to your question and context. That'll keep you in good stead.

By no means a popular formation, clumps or pileups still happen frequently. So you'll need to know how to be like an archaeologist and dig and dust your way through the strata of meaning. With any luck, you'll be able to make out the top few charms, if they're not reversed. But what lies beneath? The priest? The parrot? There's no need to let a pileup frazzle or distract you. Get your thinnest, most tapered pointer and gently begin lifting and identifying pieces. Try not to collapse the architecture; disturb it just enough to take a workable charmventory.

Remember that a charm that falls on top of another charm is blocking, suppressing, dominating, or inauspiciously influencing the bottom charm. You'll need to establish the pecking order of your pileup. What's squashing the bottom charm's mojo? What's in the middle trying to squeeze out like melted cheese? Which castmate has planted its cleats and flag on the top of that underlying charm? Given that it's so much higher than the others on the surface, does it seem like its voice (charmspeak) carries over a greater distance? There's also a flow issue with pileups, and you'll need to figure out how this relates to the narrative and your sitter.

Lines: When your charms form a line, find your beginning, and then, charm by charm, try and read this narratively, once-upon-a-charm style. Again, no two castings will ever be the same. Don't overlook the possibility that you could also find a pattern within a pattern. There are times where a combination, for example, might be embedded within the line, and those charms might want to be synthesized into a third and separate meaning—and then you move on to the next piece.

Wish Work

CASTING GRIMOIRES AND A VISION BOARD

Fill your paper with the breathings of your heart.
—William Wordsworth

I have many beautiful journals. They sit on my shelves, flanking nice books. Their spines are uncracked and their pages gleaming white, unencumbered by half-baked thoughts, chicken scrawl, or the asthmatic breathing of my heart and soul. Why? Because, neither artistic nor neat, every time my pen hovers over a virginal page, I think, *Nuh-uh: I'm gonna mess this up. I'll have to tear out pages.* I'm happy to share how I beat back this issue and discovered a practical yet magical format for a casting grimoire.

First of all, if you love charms and you haven't already, start a grimoire. It's an invaluable companion to your ever-expanding and shifting discipline. You'll be able to use it as a workbook, a place to record readings, experiences, synchronicities, and checklists. As a devoted caster, ask not what you can do for your grimoire; ask what your grimoire can do for you. Just as you'll repeatedly revisit and rework your kits, tools, technique, and approach, you'll want a journal system that can easily accommodate constant change—pages frequently inserted, removed, and reorganized. A 5-by-7 A5 six-ring binder system offers many advantages over a bound notebook including this mix of useful elements:

Six-hole loose-leaf refill paper options: blank, lined, dot or square grid. You can DIY your individual pages with washi tape, stickers, or illustrations. I've also glue-gunned mini pom-poms (and my fingers) to a few page borders.

Assorted and brightly colored tab dividers. Perfect for arranging the grimoire into chapters such as creative development pages for your kits—base, VIPs, or themed charm or word chain kits; your need it-got it checklists; charmventory; personal musings and scribbles, records, and memorable readings. The beauty of a ring binder system is that you can remove and file a year's worth of readings if you like and insert fresh paper.

Six-hole clear zipper folders. These are ideal for storing ruled or blank index cards. Create sets of *charmala fact cards* to help you recall the full range of attributes for your quadrants, houses or numerological paths, or dice, for example. Keep them by your side, then return them to their pouch after a reading.

You can create special pages and lists like a Charm Caster's Bucket List. Develop a list of casting activities that you've just gotta do. Head out into nature with a thermos of hot chocolate and throw some charms onto the forest floor. Or have a themed Midnight Margarita Casting Party. Formally and cordially invite a friend for a charmed evening that begins with a few appetizers, cocktails, or mocktails and ends with a late-night casting. Or begin a movies, TV, books, and music list. Whenever you hear something that excites your imagination, like a line of dialogue or a lyric that speaks to you personally, record it for your grimoire. This can lend profound new meaning and context to certain pieces. I noticed while watching the movie *The American* when one character asked a dancer, "*Do you want to be a prima?*" I have two ballet charms: one a ballerina on point and the other a frilly tutu. The ballerina now carries that implication of severe self-sacrifice and asks how hard will you work and how far will you go to be the best? And while the other still represents dedication and passion, it's content to be in the corps.

(Photo credit: Roger Carlsen)

Wish Work

Clear your table space—and schedule. Pull out your grimoire and craft supplies, and put your dreams on the top of the to-do list.

This is a classic example of a DIY casting divination that can be stored in a ring binder system and easily accessed for future work. Two blank pages will be bordered with and washi-taped together in the middle—hole sides out. Once folded, it fits inside your binder.

Create a Vision Board Casting Map

A vision board is your heart's collage. It's a pictorial representation of a wish, meaningful scraps of hope, and potential. In this exercise, you're going to create a very personal vision board which will become a casting map. You'll cover your pages with personally relevant images including a sigil. Once charged with manifestation magic, you'll cast your charms over its surface.

Sometimes, depending on the wish, we can get results quickly—but it can also take time or require a new or slightly revised perspective. You'll have your own special map dedicated to wish fulfillment, a casting-in-progress that you can revise and update as you like. Every time you cast on this page, the objective will be to gain more insight on how to practically take your wishes from the stuff of dreams and make them real.

YOU WILL NEED

- Scissors
- Photos, illustrations, or magazine and catalog images
- Tape—washi or Scotch. (Just a quick word: Washi tape is opaque. It holds images firmly in place yet lifts easily without tearing the page. Scotch tape, although clear, is sticky and permanent. There's no margin for changing your mind or future work. Washi tape comes in many different colors and designs and adds pop to your page.)
- A plastic or credit card. (This is the best way to cut washi tape.)
- 2 sheets of A5 loose-leaf six-ring binder paper
- A pen
- A snack
- Some wistful, faraway music

Use the two vertical blank pages as your magical canvas. Washi tape them together in the center (front and back) with their six-ring binder holes facing outward.

THE WISH SIGIL

Your first step for this project is to make a wish for the heart of your vision board. What do you want to manifest? Keep your intention focused and at least within the area code of possibility.

Begin with a sentence, for example: *I would love to own a Victorian house.* Now change this into a statement and a mindset that's assumed success: **I *live* in a Victorian house.** Invoke the certainty of the present tense: I *have* my master's degree in psychology; I *am* casting charms professionally in an old trailer on my driveway.

Write your intention here: ____

SIGILS (IN A NUTSHELL)

When petitioning the universe, you want to put your best foot forward. So on a separate sheet of paper where you can practice and make mistakes you're going to create a sigil. A sigil is a symbolic and magical representation of a wish come true. You'll design a sigil, cut it out, stick it into the circle in the middle of the blank template, and then charge it with intention.

To make your sigil, take your sentence and with a pen, begin crossing out all of the vowels. *I live in a Victorian house* becomes *LVNVCTRNHS.* Revisit this jumble of letters and cross out the repeating consonants, to wit: *LVNCTRHS.*

Your final letters: ____

Now play. Draw the *L* on the page; add the *V* at a unique angle; then blend in the *N*, and so on, until you can't recognize the letters because they've all come together to form a symbol. Don't be surprised if the sigil somehow resembles what you're asking to manifest. When you're satisfied that you have it right, cut it out and stick it in the middle of your magical canvas.

Light a candle, take a deep breath, and clear your busy mind. Stare into the flame, focus on your statement of intention, and visualize it happening. What does this feel or look like? Once you can see it in your mind's eye, redirect your gaze onto the sigil. Cast your power, passion, and will into the sigil and charge it with intention. Are the lines and curves beginning to lift, shimmy, shift, and activate? Does this symbol feel like it's taking on a life of its own? If so, now you're ready to create borders for your page, and add the images that support the visualization of the goal.

MAKE A DECORATIVE BUT MEANINGFUL FRAME

Frame your template by decorating the half to one-inch borders on all sides of the page. Washi tape is a cheap and cheerful way to pretty-up the edges. Lay half of the width of the tape over the page border and fold the other half over onto the back of the page. This makes a neater edge.

CUTTING AND PASTING

Grab a few old publications, and cut out images that evoke your understanding of the *experience* of your wish. For instance, using the example of ***I live in a Victorian house***, I found an image of a room with lead-paned windows and lace curtains to represent a parlor, a cozy and private room within which to divine and create. Other inspirations: A porch swing—a place to dream-storm beside a scented candle and a stack of books. A rosebush—blissful hours spent in nature. A pumpkin-shaped Dutch oven—cooking and entertaining with good friends. You get the idea. Now begin laying your cutouts down around the sigil. Shift them around until you get your perfect orientation, then tape them into place. How's it look? Intriguing, right?

When doing this kind of work, it's important to note that, while the *exact* wished-for Victorian home might *actually* have that parlor and porch, the universe is aligned more with the soul's expression of wants and needs and will just take it from there. You might end up manifesting a *perfect* living space that although a variation on this theme, still has those authentic characteristics you need to survive and thrive.

BEFORE WE MOVE ON: A QUICK CHECKLIST

- ☐ Pick a wish
- ☐ 2 pages glued together in the middle, hole sides outward
- ☐ Sigil designed, charged, and taped into center
- ☐ Borders decorated
- ☐ Images cut out and taped into place

Manifestation Magic

Before you begin your actual casting, you'll need to assign meanings to the various areas on your casting board. When a charm lands on your center sigil, this is a key message regarding your wish or the manifestation process. You'll also need to understand the implications of a charm falling in the other areas of your Vision Map.

You've selected each of the images on your map according to how you see yourself relating to your wish. These are your conscious desires, your surface wants and must-haves. And this is where it gets interesting. Now we're going to let your unconscious reveal *why* you've selected these images and allow these reasons to become the basis for the casting.

Make a list of your images in the chart on page 158.

In the first column, write down your original reason for selecting this picture. What is it? What aspect of your wish does it represent? Why do you want this? *Lead-paned windows and lace curtains evoke old-world, simpler-time elements of a cozy, spacious parlor, in which to divine and create.*

In the second column, look at each image again, only this time, ask yourself, *Why do I need this?* In other words, *What would this make me feel, think, or perceive as having been accomplished? Mastery. Inspiration.* What's potentially lacking in your current life or situation? *Privacy. Space. Sanctuary.* This will open a dialogue with your unconscious and reveal a deeper motivation for wanting to manifest this new reality into your life. Record this second statement in column two.

Use this information to define the areas on your Vision Map. Even if they seem far removed from the images themselves, still commit to these assignments of meaning. And they only need to make sense to you. Manifestation is affected by our unconscious motivations, and these connections will help trigger insightful and numinous information regarding the truth of what we genuinely need on a soul level.

If you don't make these connections right away, don't worry. Ponder it for a while. Relax. Walk away and let the message come to you in silence.

Using the example of the intention, *I live in a Victorian house.*

Image	1. Conscious Desire	2. Unconscious Need
Windows, lace	Parlor. Sanctuary. Privacy.	Mastery. Purpose. Occult. Creativity. Space.
Rosebush	Nostalgia. Beauty.	Grounding. Romance. Exercise.
Porch, swing	Soothing. Comfort.	Sanctuary. Slow living.
Pumpkin pot	Hearth. Friendship.	Belonging. Nurturing.

Image	1. Conscious Desire	2. Unconscious Need

Casting tips: Once your Vision Map is finished, gather your charms by your side. Before each casting, take a deep breath, and recharge your sigil. Now sprinkle—salt and pepper—a few charms over your Vision Map.

What are your charms telling you about your wish in terms of timing, alignment, suitability, challenges, resources, potential, or probability? Is there a second story emerging that requires mindful consideration before this wish can be fulfilled? Is there a hidden strength or resource that you can rely on or limitations that need to be addressed? Here's the real work: Do you really need a "Victorian house" or is it a metaphor for something else? What are you really asking for?

Note the repetition of certain words and ideas in your chart because that's something bubbling under the surface that wants conscious recognition. While you're waiting for your "Victorian house," a simple decluttering, reorganization, or cleansing of your current area could address a need for that *experience* of space. Rest assured that your charms will help connect all of these dots. Back to the future: What next steps are they recommending to land your dream? If you have to—and you'll know when—cast again and again, until that sigil says, *And... I'm... spent. You're welcome.*

Synchronicity

Always a high, when your intentions are in alignment with your soul's purpose and begin to activate, you'll experience episodes of synchronicity. Be present. Record these moments. Dedicate a page to these occurrences in your casting grimoire. And don't forget this red-letter entry:

I manifested ____________________ on this date: ____________________

> *Synchronicity is the coming together of inner and outer events in a way that cannot be explained by cause and effect and that is meaningful to the observer.*
>
> —Carl Jung

13

Practice Makes Perfect; Play Makes Perfect Practice

Ethically speaking, when divining there are a few things we should avoid. We're not doctors, so medical and mental health diagnoses are a big no-no. Respectfully advise your sitter to consult a clinical professional. Also using sacred tools as spiritual spyware—snooping into someone's life predictively without their consent—is also a low-vibrational practice. Another good chat. Now that we've established some basic ground rules, we're going to break them—but only in a highly principled way, of course.

If you don't have a revolving-door practice—client in-client out—chances are, you'll have a number of charms that won't see the light of day (or night) for a long time. They'll be loitering at the dark bottom of the bowl waiting for their cue to shine. So not only does regular practice improve every aspect of casting from technique to interpretation to personal confidence, it keeps your charms in more frequent rotation. You'll get to experience new and strange combinations with every fingerful, which is why practice is so important.

I maintain that for diviners at every skill level there's nothing more essential for growth and development than receiving constant validation. If you're reading for yourself or working with a sitter, you'll get that feedback. The first result will be you'll become your own best critic. You'll know immediately if you need to put in more work with an individual piece or make changes to your method, and your sitter will either confirm or negate your findings. Still, we all know that this is never a cut-and-dried process, because you'll have readings that will be bang on, but your sitter's awareness, openness, willingness, or timing could be subject to a deeper personal agenda, which also needs to be respected. All the more reason why you need to remain faithful to your process and prowess so that you don't melt into a miasma of self-doubt. Investing the time into really getting to know your pieces and seeing how they react in a wide and unfamiliar range of contexts will only make you a better and more confident caster.

Between or in lieu of client readings, there's an easy and playful way to practice: the news. There's no shortage of it, that's for sure. Brand spanking new and breaking, old and hotly debated, true or false, sensational and outrageous, full of juicy, audacious indictments—it doesn't matter. Throwing charms at a budding celebrity tabloid scandal, shockers such as death announcements, a criminal or legal proceeding, or politics and social unrest is a good way to test your mettle because they're all either developing or fully blown stories, which means you'll likely get what? Correct: validation. The facts will eventually emerge or can be found in existing published articles.

In the beginning, avoid familiarizing yourself with too many details of the subject of your investigation, no matter how tempting. Think like a top journalist, and prepare a line of questioning. Cast and record your interpretations, then do some follow-up research and compare notes. Keep in mind that some events or storylines can be heavy and emotionally difficult. Send blessings for all concerned if there are casualties involved before you work, and give thanks and, for your own well-being, close and clear your space and ground once finished.

The way we do all of this ethically is by staying true to this intention: *Hello, Spirit. Listen, I'm just taking the Wee Ones out on an adventure, full throttle, to push and test the boundaries of my understanding, so when the time comes for me to be called into service, I'll have the certainty and know-how to help, heal, and empower.*

It's also a wonderful way to spend quality time fortifying your connection with your helping spirit(s). No doubt, you'll discover, Spirit has its own inimitable way of expressing—and sometimes, surprisingly, a great sense of humor.

> Find a tabloid magazine and cast a few charms over the gossipy, attention-grabbing picture and headlines on the cover page. Let your charms give you an initial scoop. Did you get a validating charm or two? Well done. Your charms are attuned. Did a fly charm fall over someone's mouth? Has the word chain *NO* or *XXX* landed somewhere on the headline, on a word like *split*, *ruin*, or *alien*? What's that tell you about the accuracy or agenda of the feature story? Document your findings, then check your impressions against the tell-all article inside.

Creative Casting Surfaces: Magazines

Keep an eye out for vintage magazines. They make great casting surfaces. Playful and provocative, they're filled with irresistible ads featuring scenic human landscapes. Advertising wasn't the same in the 1950s. You'll either be shocked, disgusted, surprised, or entertained by what you see. But as a diviner, you'll more than likely be inspired. By first assessing whatever image or concept is being sold, then rescripting it through a therapeutic filter, you'll have plenty of rich layers to work with.

We all know that advertising can be an insidious art, a slick salvo of strategic messages on how one should live, think, act, look, believe, and be to belong. All of which is slyly designed to appeal to what we may already be thinking or feeling. Ads imbued with these kinds of images and narratives are, frankly, *prima materia* for getting to the root causes of a situation, dynamic, or challenge. You can cast over these wily elements and glean valuable insight into ego- or personality-based versus soul-driven aspirations.

They can also be so valuable for castings aimed at getting to the root cause of learned limitations and generational imprints that may want to be clarified and healed. In chapter 14, I'll share a sample reading in which I cast over an old *Life* magazine for a Royal Portable typewriter. It will be an eggs-to-apples run-through that will explain how to work therapeutically with this kind of content.

Bibliomancy and Stichomancy

Stichomancy, though hardly a term that rolls off the tongue, is a powerful divination that works like this: Focus on a question. Open any book. Let your finger or gaze fall on a random word, sentence, or passage. Connect with the message. Originally, its adherents would use whatever wisdom-based text was hot off the press during their day: Homer, Virgil, *Fear and Loathing in Las Vegas*, sacred manuscripts, or the Bible, in which case you'd call it bibliomancy.

You might be a credible authority, but there will still be times when your inner voice croons, *The knowledge you seek is outside of you.* And that new divine channel of communication could be a book, magazine, or online text. Some diviners prefer opening a book to a random page, then, eyes closed, they let their index finger swoop down on a word or passage like an osprey nabbing a fish. Others, eyes also closed, like to softly run their index finger up and down the page, like they're reading Braille, until they intuit, *OK, stop here.*

If and when I *stich it up*, it's usually during a reading where there's one cagey charm requiring extra work and more attention. It's all going swimmingly well, then *yikes*: an annoying speed bump. It's easy to lose your cool with a "Listen *you*, balloon poodle dog, I know what you should mean—*I animated you!*" Or wonder, *Should I just bluff my way through this bit?* It's not your strongest option.

Chances are you're missing a subtle facet of that piece. When something remains elusive, something important, *keep seeking*. Obviously, this isn't a viable technique for a performative or one-on-one casting with a sitter, but if you have the time and luxury, give this a whirl.

Allow yourself to be drawn to a charged source. This could be a book, magazine, or the result of a Google search. Inevitably, it will yield something that you haven't considered, but Spirit really wanted you to know. Soft scan the text and wait for that charged sentence or passage, the message that raises off the page. You'll know you've hit it when you flood with a strong sense of recognition. Your inner voice confirms, *Yup!—that's exactly what I meant or needed*—the missing link. If you don't find it immediately, search for another source. Once you've been called, trust that it's out there. You'll know it when it finds you.

Lost and Found Chart: Objects and Subjects

In my household, items are lost, misplaced, and ostensibly carted off by naughty Fae with alarming regularity. Rather than waste precious time, energy, and little gray cells tearing apart your home to find car keys (inanimate, object of your search) or, say, a missing animal (animate, subject of a search), try this Lost and Found Chart. Let's find those MIAs.

Randomly select nine charms, one at a time, and lay them in order, from one to nine into this classic square of nine chart. Use right-side-up charms only for this session. It may take some time to understand how the charms are expressing. Just be patient. Once you start seeing results, you'll be relieved to have this in your arsenal of techniques (and grimoire). If you're having difficulty interpreting any of your charms, remember you can always *stich it up*.

Lost and Found Chart

1. What's KNOWN Visualize the missing object or subject. If it's a subject, you can also place something that belongs to them here. This is a piece of information that floods a spotlight on the MIA. Charms 1 and 5 tag team.	**2. I am NOT here** So stop looking already! What does this rule out for you?	**3. The Losing** Valuable info connected to how the MIA went missing. State of mind? Circumstances? Anything that could twig key facts. If you were the last person to handle or see the subject or object, you may have an unconscious memory that, once massaged, allows you to retrace your steps.
4. Action Do this! This is your first step, a key action that assists in your search and the finding (if it's meant to be). If it's not, this may offer additional info or guidance. Also glance at charm 7.	**5. Object or Person** This offers a present perspective on the MIA. Pay attention to the way the charm has chosen to nuance this message similarly, differently, or progressively from charm 1.	**6. The Finding** AHA! Hello. I'M HERE. You may need to backtrack to this. It likes to tag team with charms 7 and 8 to direct you to the location or reveal any potential issues with the search.
7. What's Being Overlooked? What aren't you considering? What's hidden in plain sight?	**8. What's Next to Me?** Because something has to be. What's next to the MIA. This is a good clue. Like charm 2, this helps rule out bad leads.	**9. The Homecoming** Charm 6 is the location; charm 9 has its own message and mission—maybe about the losing or the finding or a future plan to help with this happening again. Read with charm 6.

Sample Lost and Found Reading: Where's the Neighbor's Cat?

Notice the different voices in this sample reading. Each piece has its own charm-speak, a unique way of expressing, literal or metaphoric. Some of these charms are even being cheeky. No surprise here given the nature of this reading—as you'll soon see. Sometimes a piece will blurt it out clear as day: *Get it? Got it! Good.* Or it communicates via a familiar idiom, or phrase. Other times, it's just a vehicle for a psychic impression. When this happens, you'll see that its sole purpose is to become a springboard that lets you swan dive into a deep body of meaning.

1. **Doghouse RX (known).** *Very funny. Only recently, after many years, the neighbor's cat is no longer allowed to come into our house. He sits outside every day. Being in the "doghouse" is an idiom for being in trouble—both of us. I know this.*
2. **Three rings (not here).** *There are three animals next door: two dogs and the cat. Kitty's not at his own home. Don't look for him there.*
3. **Ferris wheel (the losing).** *Change is a big factor in this MIA's migratory patterns.*
4. **Ladder (action).** *Take a few steps to find him. And he's up somewhere, at a height.*
5. **Red rose (present).** *The color red is significant: he's safe, surrounded by beauty or flowers.*
6. **Unicorn (I'm here. The finding).** *In a magical place.*
7. **Cathedral (Overlooked).** *The neighbor's house, which is for sale, has a tall peaked roof, like a cathedral. It's been experiencing big changes, including a new, young, and energetic puppy, lots of downsizing, open houses and workmen.*
8. **Espresso Moka (Next to this).** *Oh, you clever charms. I have an espresso here at my desk.*
9. **Saw (supports the finding).** *Again, very funny. Sawing wood is an idiom for snoring.*

Synthesis: Where's the neighbor's cat? OK, so this was a trick question, because I knew the answer. I know it's cheating, still this is also how you can practice and play to see how the Wee Ones rise to the occasion. And they sure did. The kitty's snoring blissfully, in my magical office, beside my desk covered with a floral tablecloth. He's curled up in a red sweatshirt, up on a couch, just steps away from my latte (and his home, the "cathedral" next door). The rose, three rings, cathedral, and Ferris wheel suggest that he's experienced a change of routine; he's (briefly) sought cozy sanctuary where he can relax and be the sole center of attention away from the two dogs. He'll be lovingly escorted out soon . . . when it stops pouring rain . . . just saying, because that doghouse vibe is real.

The Yes/No, Soon/Delay Casting: A Themed Kit

This is a specialty kit. It's a casting system that will help you get those answers to close-ended questions—because sometimes enquiring minds just want to know. This layout was bigheartedly inspired by Barbara Moore and her book *Tarot Spreads,* but has since been recruited for the Wee Ones as well. You can either make a themed word chain or (VIP) charm kit to use in tandem with base kit charms. As it's helped me, many a time, may it guide you through your own decision-making.

Create a Yes/No Word Chain Set

For this specialty yes/no themed kit, this is sample checklist of word chains. Feel free to reword or rename them to your own specific needs and preferences. These act like look-at-me pieces. You'll also be casting a few base kit charms around them to add supporting details to your definitive answer—yes or no, soon or delay. Keep this theme kit in its own labeled tin.

Make or Assign These Five Primary Pieces

Yes—Right away, a sure thing

No—Sorry, not happening at this time, or at all.

Soon—Hold on; it's a coming. Minor hiccup.

Delay—Significant obstacle has to be overcome first.

Answer—Find a special look-at-me charm, a crystal, or . . .? Wherever it lands, that's your answer.

Make and Assign These Secondary Pieces

Act—An outcome requires an action.

Exit—Go. Release. Direct your energy elsewhere. You may have dodged a bullet.

Head—Use reason. How are your thoughts affecting an outcome?

Heart—Follow your bliss. How are your emotions affecting this outcome?

Clue—The game's afoot, Sherlock. A piece of information you need to factor in.

Wow—Better or worse than you imagined.

Align—An issue of alignment. Go back to source.

Seek—Read the fine print. Keep researching, reading, investigating.

XXX—Yikes. Heads-up. Red flag. Augments negativity.

♥♥♥ (or YYY)—It's all good. A hug or high five. Augments positivity. Mitigates negativity.

Lay down a single-colored quick-pull surface. Isolate the answer piece and place it aside. Ready the four remaining primary pieces, a small container holding the secondary pieces, and another with your base kit of charms. Set up your primary word chains like this:

YES	SOON
DELAY	NO

1. Focus on a question.
2. In your hands, add and mix one to three randomly selected secondary word chains, the same amount of base kit charms, and the answer piece.
3. Just go ahead and cast. Or, for added control, blindly parcel out the pieces in your hands in four little groups. Cast one small group over YES, another over NO, then SOON, and last DELAY.
4. Look to see where your answer piece has landed.

If your answer charm has landed clearly on or closest to one of the four—that's your thumbs-up or thumbs-down. If it's somewhere in the middle in no-man's-land, scrutinize the charmscape. No answer is sometimes an answer. Maybe it's not the right time or place to know. Maybe the question needs to be refocused. You know how to do this.

SAMPLE READING USING THE ANSWER PIECE, TWO SECONDARY WORD CHAINS, AND TWO CHARMS

Will I (finally) receive my package today?

The answer piece landed just beside SOON, and all of my other pieces were smothering it. My handcuffs charm was entwined with the Act chain. The Clue chain landed outside of my small casting area with my flattery (RX) charm. The package isn't coming today; my hands are tied. There's nothing I can do to receive my package today. The sender can't say anything reassuring other than it's en route. What needs to be factored in is that because of the way she sent it, she also has no control to fix this. It's coming from outside of the EU. Soon is a function of yes, but it's an affirmative with complications. I didn't get that package, but a new one was sent and didn't take long to arrive. See? Clean. Easy. Now I'm totally free to fret about something new.

Higher-Stakes Dice: Stop. Yield. Go.

I'm sure by now you have at least one die in your main casting kit. If not, note to self... If you're ready and willing to bump up some creative stakes, try this: find three small dice—green, yellow, and red—signifying go, yield, and stop respectively. Here again are some basic meanings for single die numbers 1–6:

1. Self. New beginnings.
2. Partnership. Commitments.
3. Expansion. Creativity. Something added.
4. Foundation. Structure. Status quo. Tradition.
5. Chaos. Change. Rowdy fun.
6. Victory. Harmony.

Should one or more of these traffic-light die present in a casting, think of it like you're approaching an intersection in your life and need to make a decision. Green advises to keep on trucking; you can also make a turn, go in another direction, actively pursue another path. Yellow cautions to slow down—or alternatively, give something a final but very cautious and focused burst of energy. Red is stop; road closed. Note the color, number, as well as any neighboring castmates to get more clarification on what these signs are telling you.

We'll all have our own way of intuiting these dice/color/charm combinations; these are just examples: **yellow-5**: *An unexpected complication delays progress*, or *an event or friend's party might be delayed or rescheduled*. If a bell or another red flag charm falls next to this die, it could be alerting you to slow down and reconsider some aspect of this invitation. If, however, you roll a **red-5** that touches or is near a bell: *Stay home. Trouble's afoot.*

If two dice present in a larger casting, or even three—and it's always possible—what do you do? It might be tempting to add the numbers and reduce the result to a single number, but in this particular instance, it's best to keep it simple. Read each die separately, then if it feels right, synthesize the messages. For example, **green-1** lands in the sixth house (career) of your charmala (or next to a VIP career significator). *A new beginning (possibly an offer for a new job) is a go.* **Red-5** lands in the bracelet with the lion charm and an American penny, heads up. Remember, heads on an American penny is Abraham Lincoln, which represents the boss, and tails is the Lincoln Memorial or later designs, meaning the workplace or building. *It's clearly time* (inside bracelet) *to summon the courage* (lion) *to collapse* (5) *and stop* (red) *a situation, meaning tender resignation to your direct boss* (penny).

If that penny had landed tails or building side up, it would still suggest the resignation, but from the actual company or physical building. Is it possible this job offer is coming from another department within or location within the same firm? What do you think?

From the Egg to the Apples

TWO SAMPLE READINGS—METHOD AND MUSINGS

Creative without strategy is called art.
Creative with strategy is called advertising.
—Jef I. Richards

Sample Casting 1 for a Male Sitter: Prep, Casting, and Synthesis

As mentioned earlier, old magazines can make superlative casting surfaces. While flipping through a 1957 *Life* magazine, I found this ad for Royal Portable typewriters. It checked all of the right boxes: bold colors, sparse design elements, and the right size. And what fine diviner wouldn't instantly be drawn to a three-panel layout with built-in past, present, and future features? Add slick ad copy and relatable characters with big expressions, emotions, and agendas and ta-da: the inane can easily be adapted to the arcane. The ad claims that a Royal Portable can not only help your kid with spelling and accuracy, but

Lucky boy!
with honors this year
new Royal Portable!

also "add that important touch of fun" to homework, which ostensibly causes improvement and achievement.

The first panel introduces the main character: a boy laboring over homework looking stuck, bored, confused, and weary. The second panel portrays the same boy, his back to the audience, standing and facing a stern father and a despairing mother. *Oh oh! To be a fly on the wall for this earful.* In the third and last panel, the denouement of our story, the boy is back at his desk. Only, he's smiling brightly, sitting in front of—*what now*? That's right. It's a brand spanking new typewriter. He's wearing a graduation gown and holding his cap high. At its most basic, this panel's selling the idea of an action that can spark auspicious change. This map's ideal for exploring the inner and outer nature and cause of a challenge and its potential resolution and solution. It can explore a balance between work and play; on a deeper level, it can ask, *From what ideas, beliefs, behavior have you really graduated?*

Studying Anatomy: The Flesh and Bones of a Casting Map

Before I cast any charms, I study, customize, and prepare my divination in baby steps. This is how I settle into an approach.

Contemplation and analysis of the ad's design and hot spots. Make mental notes on the available design elements, and then assign a layer of personal meanings. What design elements catch your eye? What are the *hot spots*? The boy's hand holding a pen; the mother's hand that grips her son's shoulder. What will it mean if a charm lands on someone's leg, foot, or head, the typewriter, or the graduation cap? How will I convert these hot spots into questions that the charms can answer? Let's say a charm lands on the boy's backside. It begs this question: What's it going to take for my sitter to get off their backside? And if that charm was a shoe or a boot? The potential interpretation: a good ol' kick in the pants.

Adapt the ad into a divination. There are three panels with not only a built-in timeline of past, present, and future, but also dramatic structure. How can this inform the casting? The boy will represent the main significator (you or your sitter); it's his story, and there's a character arc. He's grown and changed from the first to third panel. What are the charms saying about the sitter's evolution?

Clearly, these postwar parents are exerting loving but dutiful pressure for him to do better or to maybe take advantage of opportunities that they didn't have. The boy's parents are secondary significators. This panel also represents external influences that have a direct impact on a main significator; mom and dad can represent actual parents. If so assigned, charms that land there can provide useful insight into how the sitter's childhood might still be seeking expression. Or mom and dad can be other key secondary significators or the role of environment on the sitter—or all of the above.

And what sparks this change? What does *graduation* really mean? The actualization of a goal—or self? That's a lot to work with. Naturally, as a diviner, you'll use the ad's storyline as a template and intuit questions that will create a therapeutic and predictive divination. Once this is done, your charms can step forward to reveal why your main significator is stuck, how they can get out of the mire, and how their conflict can be best resolved. What are the working influences that need to be tabled? What action can they take? How will they achieve their goal? How does it end?

> *A little girl bought a balloon for her brother. George watched.*
> *He felt curious again. He felt he MUST have a bright red balloon.*
> —H.A. Rey—*Curious George*

Line dancing: interpretive body copy. Print advertisements, like a children's book, have a much lower word count than a novel, so *every* word selected must be the *perfect* word. The agenda will be convincing and clear. Review the copy and also read (and feel) between the lines. What are the words selling, implying, promising? This is where you'll find your pivotal theme and the context for your divination. Write a short list. *Rekindling spark. Improvement. Graduation/honors.* Are there specific words that feel more charged than others? A headline that's a hot spot? *Lucky Boy.* Maybe your charms won't land on any of these, but you'd best be prepared. (See Murphy's law, p. 76.) Now, soft gaze the story for its liminality, and create your own divine approach. Begin customizing. Create a list of working questions for each area, panel, ad copy, and hot spots that will direct your focus through the divination. You'd be surprised how intuitively and quickly, if not instantly, this can be done.

The Casting: Tools, Technique, and Gung Ho Attitude

- I begin with the less-pointy cocktail stirrer, which has a bulbous crystal on top. I run the pretty teardrop around the inside of a plain jumpmala to help me shape it into a rectangle border around the page.

- For this casting, I randomly pulled three VIP charms (three panels), then selected two small fingerfuls of casting charms. One side of the brain, I guess, gauges the size of the surface, while the other's feeling it out in the charm bowl. Eyes closed, I felt the base kit bracelet hook on to my finger, so it wanted to come out. Pieces all go into a blind bowl. They're gently mixed, poured into my hand, then sprinkled over the page.

- I find the look-at-me pieces. I want to see what life area/hot topics have landed. I check to see if anything's inside the bracelet and where and how it's presented. I study the charmscape for jumpers, loners, and patterns; validating charms, like-minded pieces; charms that support the theme; flow, directionality, and indirect communication. While I might make surface notes, I remain more or less detached—until I pick up my (pointy) pointer. This is a personal ritual. This is my way of signaling that I'm ready for deeper engagement. Well, almost. After the unavoidable *WTF* moment, I breathe. All good. I switch from ego to faith and trust that I'll be guided to the charms that are tasked with getting this narrative up and running.

The Reading

Sitter and question: A creative and typically productive man feels debilitated by a motivational crisis. *What's the nature of the block and how can he graduate past it?*

Look-at-me charms: Bird (alignment, freedom, authenticity), **Shell** (energy, life force), **Crystal cube** (manifestation, tangible result), **Bracelet** (look here).

FIRST PANEL

Copy: *Last year at this time he was barely getting by in school.*
Working questions: In what way is the sitter struggling to *get by*? How is stagnation, frustration, or doubt being potentially experienced? What's the homework, the goal or project? What's already known (past) about this situation?

Charm: Cat and Mouse
Area: On the boy's lower face
Interpretation: This could literally be seen as the cat bringing a mouse, sustenance, or a gift to the boy. It doesn't resonate. This felt, instead, like the cat chasing the mouse, an experience that resulted in weakening or exhaustion and the fear of defeat. Likely, this involved a relationship or partnership with a power dynamic. Yet the sitter has taken this all "on the chin" and endured with stoicism and without complaint or expression. (Had the cat and mouse fallen on the throat—he'd have spoken up.) *The sitter is chewing on the old dynamics of a relationship or partnership instead of focusing on his goal.*

Charm: Trophy (#1)
Area: Over the heart
Interpretation: The sitter is no stranger to accomplishment; he must know this in his heart. He's already achieved something laudable, and no one can take this away. This sitter aims high. He's ambitious but also thrives with appreciation and recognition—but he won't admit it. The #1 feature on the trophy feels charged. I read this as a separate symbol that suggests that the sitter may be currently working independently, and any goal-related struggles may have

to do with allowing himself to depend solely on #1—himself. Also, it doesn't escape my notice that the trophy charm is kindred to the idea of *graduation. The sitter already knows how to succeed; he just needs to keep his eye on the prize.*

Charm: Racoon (RX); leg
Area: On the homework over writing hand directly under the boy's gaze; this line of charms continues into the second panel (present and external influences).
Interpretation: The racoon is reversed and upside down. It's nestled comfortably into the crook of a bent leg. (This piece means *next steps forward.*) These charms form a line that continues into the second panel. At this stage, I'm only dealing with the first-panel charms.

The racoon and the top of the leg have fallen on the image of a hand holding a pen. When charms land directly on hot spots, they activate that primary layer of meaning, for example, the writing hand (work, productivity, creativity). Is this auspicious? Inauspicious? It now depends on the charm. I love racoons, but in my kit, this little fellow carries a bit of both thief and trickster energy. (If, presenting right-side-up, his mask were showing, this would bring out different qualities, like intentional sneakiness.) Still, whatever charm touches this bandit is what's been pinched from the sitter.

It also occurs that racoons love abandoned spaces. What's that say about the leg's activity? What then can be interpreted about the sitter's forward motion? Correct. He's immobilized. The sitter admits to being drained of impetus, but also oddly finds solace in this inertia (the racoon is cozy), at least for the moment.

The boy's staring down at the charms that have fallen on his writing hand; the sitter acknowledges that he's gone through a runaround (cat and mouse) with a "superior" (cat), an experience that's "robbed" him (racoon) of his signature keep-calm-and-carry-on resilience (leg). We all know that cats have an innate predatory drive and will always out-strategize and inveigle whoever identifies as the mouse in this game. There's a blessing in this lesson, and the charms remind the sitter of the need to claim his worth and stature.

The sitter's spirit and confidence regarding a goal is flagging, and there are notable motivational and energetic issues at the heart of a struggle to "get by."

Charms: Carnelian, siren, race car (RX), (VIP) golden bird (alignment, freedom, authenticity)
Area: At the boy's feet
Interpretation: There's an overturned race car (speed, progress, and movement, RX) and a small carnelian stone (stress and burnout) sitting on desk legs (support). The car (front end shows direction) was racing toward the siren (temptation), but crashed. The siren is now tail over teakettle, sinking silently, serenely downward, presumably back into her lair. The car's flipped over, and the *siren's song*, fading. That's key. Her head points directly to the off-panel word *was*. I ask the sitter if he's been engaging in any "self-soothing," and how's that been working for him? 'Nuff said.

This cluster of charms landed at the bottom of the panel, on the boy's feet. They feel like weights. I observe that there are multiple signs—the images of the writing hand and feet, as well as charms, the car (RX) and racoon-inhabited leg—that reinforce a theme of impeded movement, energy, and progress. The golden (VIP) bird (beauty of freedom, authenticity, and alignment), however, feels highly charged. It's soaring away from the drama of these heavier charms and toward a golden prediction at the bottom of the page: *graduation* and *honor*. The sitter's reminded that he's working on something he's meant to do and that the way he's been numbing and avoiding (siren sinking into the depths) is contributing more to the problem than the solution. This is also supported by the fact that the siren's head is pointing directly to the word *was*. Isn't it time to consign this behavior to the past?

> *Shut up, she tells her monkey mind. Please shut up, you picker of nits, presser of bruises, counter of losses, fearer of failures, collector of grievances future and past.*
> —Leni Zumas, *Red Clocks*

In order to regain his momentum, the sitter needs a new and improved GPS, a fresh course, a redirection of thoughts, behavior, and beliefs (unworthiness) that can help him change his neural pathways. There are times the heart needs to triumph over the head. A more heart-centered approach to his work will remind him that he loves what he does. Instead of wasting precious energy on retracing steps, he needs to put his needs and goals first. He'll discover fuel, freedom, and direction moving forward by reconnecting with and trusting his soul purpose; this helps him soar above this tailspin, way, way up where the oxygen and vibration are rarified.

SECOND PANEL

Copy: *Dad lectured. Mom pleaded. But nothing seemed to spark a light.*

Working questions: What are the external influences? Is there a perception of pressure? Is it internal or external? Who are you doing this for? What isn't working for you? How's your inner spark? Where might it have gone, why, and how can it be rekindled?

Charms: (VIP) shell (energy, life force, flow), bullet casing, part of the bracelet. The head of a snake (RX) slithering in from the third panel.

Area: Starting at the racoon from the previous panel and moving across and down through the father (lecturing, discipline), the tip of the shell ends at the bullet casing which lands at the boy's feet. Part of the bracelet falls at the mother's feet and covers the bottom of the well charm.

Interpretation: The second panel reveals that the sitter's also being triggered (bullet casing) in his environment. The direction of the shell (wide end up, tip down) reveals how his chi or energy is being utilized. It's not flowing upward to his Highest Good. Nor is it flowing toward the achievement and success hot spots in the third panel. It's draining into the bullet casing.

In a line beginning at the racoon (thief) the shell's landed on the father (critical); this character doesn't vibe like a parent, but a key second significator in the sitter's life. This character's body language feels charged, particularly his lower half (where the shell and casing have landed). His feet are about a foot apart and pointing outward, firmly and confidently planted. This character is tasked with lecturing, reprimanding, moaning and groaning, and he's not budging in his stance. So how's the sitter reacting to this stimulus? The shell's tip points to the answer: exhausting, rapid-fire reactionary outbursts. (Remember that this casing is empty; the propellant or gunpowder in the bullet has combusted. I have a complete bullet in my kit, so this piece is nuanced differently.)

The sitter admits that he and his partner have been sharing fiery exchanges. I hover my pointer over the casing to determine the bullet's trajectory. This also adds an interesting layer of information. Based on the direction of the casing, the shot would have to have been fired from the first panel and the car, siren, carnelian cluster. I ask, respectfully, if the sitter's partner has been expressing frustration or worry lately by anything that he's been doing. The sitter smiles and confirms his partner's been very supportive but is also losing patience with his *woe-and-wine-arama* habit.

It's clear that the sitter needs to manage his spark and emotions more efficiently.

Charm: The head of a snake slithering in from the third panel.
Area: Slithering out from under the typewriter in the third panel, laying on top and outside of the bracelet and touching the woman secondary significator's leg.
Interpretation: Another secondary significator, represented by the ad's mother character, is known to the sitter and connected to his work/goal. She can't entirely be trusted. The snake is low in the panel, so *in the grass*, but reversed which makes it less threatening. I just feel like this person is mildly deceptive. She's like a Pez white lie dispenser. It feels like she speaks with a forked tongue, and the sitter may never be told the truth. Still, he really doesn't need to worry about this; the snake doesn't fall inside of the bracelet; in fact, the bracelet acts like a protective boundary. *This woman can say or think whatever she pleases; it can't hurt the sitter. Besides, she's such a fraidy snake, he'll never know.*

THIRD PANEL

Copy: *Then he got a new Royal Portable. And wow, what an improvement.*
Working questions: What's the key to success? What does "graduation" and improvement look or feel like? What can you expect?

Charms: (VIP) earth crystal in the center of the bracelet (manifestation, tangible result)
Area: In front of the main significator, settled at the bottom of the panel, centered in the bracelet
Interpretation: Wow. How amazing. Whatever falls inside of the bracelet wants your attention right away. That charm is a crystal cube, the symbol of earth, manifestation. The sitter has a series of free-will choices to make to allow for this divinely happy ending, but here it is: a tangible result.

The sitter can and will complete his project. And it feels really good!

Charm: Snake (RX)
Area: Underneath the typewriter and slithering back to its owner in the second panel.
Interpretation: Bye-bye, snake. Don't let the carriage return hit you on the way out . . .
Charm: Pink flamingo (upside down)
Area: The boy's chin rests on the underside of the pink flamingo.
Interpretation: This charm, a second bird totem, brings the touch of fun that, according to the body copy, results in the improvement that leads to graduation and honors. The main significator's chin is resting on a feathery shelf, visibly back in a more comfortable, supportive, and happy place. The flamingo carries two messages for the sitter. The first is that he needs to put work and play in perspective. Due to the isolating nature of his work, his social life may have been moved to the back burner. He should try and hook up with his—I love this—*flamboyance*, which is the collective noun for more than one

flamingo. The sitter also confides that his work strays wildly from convention and he's harbored deep concerns that it wouldn't be accepted or lauded by his dusty academic peers. This charm says, *Hello! You do the true YOU.* It gives him every assurance that he's on the right path. He'll do well to bring some whimsy and personality to his own work and embrace his own colorful style.

OFF-PANEL AND CHARMS THAT FALL BELOW THE THREE PANELS

While I didn't feel that the mother and father figure in the ad represented the sitter's parents or his childhood influences, I opened up a dialogue with the charms that lay underneath the panels and looked to see if anything fell on *father lectured* or *mother pleaded.* I was also interested in anything that fell on the headline, *Lucky Boy.* Or the copy: *He'll graduate with honours this year thanks to a new Royal Portable.* (Note the use of the future tense here—*he will*—which really supports predictive work.) These are all hot spots. As the reader, you'll have to intuit your way through this landscape and be guided as to what calls you and park what doesn't.

Here's what I found:

Working Questions: What indirect conscious or unconscious influences might be affecting the sitter? What does the sitter need to understand about their childhood that still might be expressing in their adult lives? What does my sitter need to know moving forward? What helps him *graduate* past his current limitations?

Charms: (VIP) bracelet (pay attention to this), a well
Area: Over ad copy *mom pleaded*, below second panel
Interpretation: The bracelet, because of how it's landed, isn't done and has more to say. It lays on the lower part, the deepest feature of the well charm. Through a filter of my own life experience, I understand that the charm is saying he'll need to "go to the well." This expression means that whenever you feel that you've got nothing left and your conscious resources have seemingly run dry, you'll need to descend deeper, tapping into that limitless reservoir

of self and creativity. He's got to try harder to draw this inspiration from the groundwater. *He's got all the resources that he needs; he has what it takes.*

Charm: Cricket
Area: Over ad copy *dad lectured*, below second panel
Interpretation: The cricket, my auspicious bringer of luck, blocks all of these words. I ask my sitter about his father. Was he strict, encouraging, or . . .? My sitter acknowledges that his dad worked hard and was meticulous at whatever he did. He's reminded that he's got his dad's discipline, inspirational work ethic, and pride at a job well done, and that he'll reconnect with that strength.

Charm: Mother and child charm
Area: Overlapping the word *graduate* below and between second and third panel
Interpretation: The word *graduate* is charged. It's seminal to this reading. It's what the sitter needs to overcome to evolve past his challenge. I've also noted that when the bullet casing appears, it might be alerting me to the *possibility* of shrapnel, emotional, spiritual, or otherwise. The mother and child charm right side up is my charm of nurturing, perhaps a single mother and child. Reversed, it means abandonment, real or perceived. My sitter understands this. We discuss why it's so important for him to validate himself by pats on back! We consider why he identified as the mouse, and how he can outmaneuver the dynamic represented by the cat. Also why he might have had higher and unreasonable expectations for the snake. Once recognized, he was able to move on to the next charm with a much lighter and happier heart.

Charm: Mortar and pestle
Area: Over ad copy *graduate*
Interpretation: The pestle will grind, destroy, alter, and transform anything inside of its mortar into powder. This immediately echoes the empty bullet casing and its lack of propellant (metaphor for what propels us forward). This is a beautiful example of the way that charms will communicate to each other

from different areas of the casting surface. This is the sitter's new propellant. He needs to repurpose the old so that he can move forward and graduate to new honors. Only the sitter can determine what this means to him, situationally, spiritually, physically, psychologically or professionally. Our job, as readers, is to help activate that sacred process.

Sample Casting 2: Using a Wheel of Life Charmala

This reading has a lot going on. I kept this casting open for a few days. Every revisiting yielded a new cache of insight and details that had eluded me on a previous pass. There aren't enough pages to get into all of it; I will, however, blow out a few sections, and in doing so, try and give you an example of the sheer wealth of information that a few beads on a cord, a bowl of trinkets, and a vintage hankie can reveal.

Scribble

If you can't accommodate an open casting for too long, snap a picture and print it out. Infinitely more portable, you can use this to keep charm-obsessing in bed or at a coffee shop. It can then find a place in your grimoire for posterity. Oh, and never bring a porcupine quill into bed. You don't want to hear that story . . .

Love, Romance, and Relationship Reading for C and S

THE QUESTION AND BRIEF BACKSTORY

The sitter, C, had a falling out with her friend, S. The incident involved a third party. Attempts to talk it out failed, and in this snapshot of a moment, their relationship is strained. *What's really going on here? How, if possible, can these two good friends mend their broken fences?*

METHOD, SYSTEM, AND PREP

Tools: Charms, VIPs, Wheel of Life charmala with matching seer's eye, 12-by-12 cloth, preselected main and secondary significator alphabet charms *C* and *S* (Had the first names shared the same initial, I would have made word chains), twelve astrological tokens (or zodiac charms) laid outside of the charmala to boldly mark the houses, four red hearts placed outside the circle at the corners of the cloth.

Special Intentions: Two-month forecast, clockface, astrological house meanings, numbered paths, jumpers landing by the hearts take on the following layers of additional meaning:

Bottom right: To will. This requires determination and perseverance.

Top left: To dare. Step out of this comfort zone.

Top right: To learn. Or risk repeating this pattern or lesson.

Bottom left: To keep still. Resist this action.

The Castmates: Six randomly selected VIPs (six letters in friend; six represents harmony and peace), two fingerfuls of charms, two significator letters *C* and *S*.

FIRST GAZE

There aren't any *whole* charms in the seer's bull's-eye. Interesting. I check the proximity of the **C** and **S** pieces to the center and from one another. I note what falls between them. There are no jumpers, so no charms touching the hearts; four pieces touch the bracelet. Two VIPs present at the top. They form a line with another castmate.

The VIPs are the **bell** (alarm), the **coffee cup** (a break, or literally coffee, which in this case is a huge validating charm), **beer stein** (joyful social interaction), **cold heart** (emotional block, disconnect), **triangle** (core ideals), and the red **cardinal** (tutelary, presence of highest-good guidance).

WHERE TO START?

I hover a pointer over the pieces touching the bracelet and begin identifying patterns. I'm drawn to three charms at the top of the reading. They form a line: (VIP) **cardinal,** (VIP) **cold heart, cat.**

Cardinal (tutelary, highest-good guidance) is perched in Capricorn. It's also at 11 o'clock facing 12 o'clock (completion before a new beginning). For starters, when this helping spirit presents, something wants to be learned that's greater and deeper than the surface issue. Secondly, at 11 o'clock, it's heralding a necessary transition. Cold heart points, like a planchette, to the ninth house (deeper understanding and meaning). The cat (independence) is reversed and upside down. Its paws tread along path 1 (self, beginnings), and (follow the head) it's moving toward the cold heart.

The cardinal (gaze) is communicating indirectly with the topsy-turvy cat (gaze). The cold heart sits in the middle and acts like a barrier between this helping spirit and the cat. This pattern feels like it's *reigning* over the rest of the casting.

The sitter will have to work through an emotional block before a new cycle can begin. The experience of newly found independence (cat) isn't sitting well with C. Having gone through a horrible breakup, it's confirmed that this is a very sore point for her at the moment. She misses being part of a couple.

The significator pieces have both landed close to the perimeter, but because they're look-at-mes, I want to follow their lines back into the empty seer's eye to read from their perspective. And then, I'll study how the pattern radiates from the middle and out toward a conclusion. In this case, the letters almost feel like exclamation points at the end of their sentences: **C** and **S** are both standing firm in their respective narratives.

Working from the center: (VIP) **bell** has literally swallowed a **teapot** (calm, serenity). I synthesize this combination as *alarmist.* There was an overreaction or a triggered reaction. It sits on top of a loose, flapping RX **necktie** (too active or not present). **Bell** is a busy charm lending its meaning to more than one pattern. It belongs to the S storyline. It also begins a separate storyline heading to (VIP) **beer stein, coffee cup, owl RX**. Then stein has its own tale to tell. These stories are separate but all linked to the inciting incident. I'll get there in a few minutes.

S line: (S, lady, triangle, harp RX, necktie RX, bell/teapot). White-haired lady (mother or smother, well-intentioned). She clutches a handbag full of what's held dear. It's snapped shut. Nonnegotiable. **Lady** is a busy charm too. It lies horizontally and radiates barrier energy in three directions: 1) between the S and C pieces (*S has set firm boundaries*), 2) between S and the **ace of spades** (no! negativity), which belongs to C's line (*S's boundaries keep her away from what she perceives as C's negativity*), 3) between S and **triangle** (core ideals). Now Lady acts like a ceiling. On principle, S will only go so far entertaining, engaging with or trying to understand what has happened.

Lady leads to triangle (core ideals). Following the directionality of the triangle, the top corner points to something interesting. The tip lies on a reversed **harp** (harmony, angelic vibes). Harp touches reversed **necktie** on the right and **ace of hearts** on the left. Harp RX is energetically kindred to the necktie RX, both closed to the loving energy of the ace of hearts. *It's like . . . I won't and can't even go there. S's beliefs and boundaries, in that isolated incident, may have inhibited a more compassionate response to C's needs. S isn't hardwired for conflict or drama, and so it seems she wasn't as present for C in the way that my sitter would have liked. C admits she was upset. C tried to talk to S, but felt that the conversation was one-sided and entirely on S's terms.*

So what on earth happened? Let's press on. This line (**bell/teapot, stein, coffee cup, owl RX**) hugs the outside perimeter of the bracelet with two charms touching it, one of which, **bell**, is a VIP. This will be an integral storyline. The triggered **bell/teapot** reaction seems connected to a joyful social interaction (beer stein), followed by coffee? *What?* **Coffee cup** first landed on top of **owl** reversed. Turns out coffee cup is literal. It's a huge validating charm. Owl sees in the dark but it's reversed, so this means blindsided. *C had called S to* *do something; S had plans to meet another friend at a local coffee bar, but then also extended an invitation to C to come join them. C, feeling more vulnerable than usual, reacted emotionally to S's unavailability.*

Stein has its own path and story (**stein, lighthouse, lady in red RX**). **Lighthouse** (navigational aid through bad visibility, a heads-up) touches the beer stein (joyful social interaction). **Lady in red** (temptress, interfering third party) lies face down, the *base* (not the beacon) of a lighthouse is on her head. *These charms merely point out that while this coffee date may have been an unwanted development, this third party had no idea of the lay of the land and presented no ill will.*

Moving on there are the **Beefeater** (duty), upside down, and **rings** (serious commitment) in the fourth house, Cancer (home, family, emotions). These charms kind of glance off the bottom of another pattern, a curved line above, and drifting downward, feel like fallout, shrapnel. *C and S have shared a close bond. They live close to each other, and they've shared a lot over the years. C is currently questioning her role, duty, acts of service within all of her relationships. C shares that, in general, she's tired of "performing" and having to be someone she isn't in order to be understood.*

In line with the cup, two castmates, **candlestick** (illumination) and **courage ring** lie in the sixth house, Virgo, which reinforces the concepts of service to others and overcoming obstacles that are standing in the way of personal success and achievement. Like the owl and the lighthouse, a candlestick also represents seeing in the dark. And what is courage, really? It's having to do something that you don't want or think, in the moment, that you can do. *There's an emerging theme for C. Healing (cold heart) that involves facing difficult truths coming to light about who she is outside of the context of a relationship.* S, Lady in red and coffee cup are all agents of this important breakthrough.

C combination and cluster: (horse and cart/C, playing card aces, boot, citrine) No surprise here, **C** lands in the first house, Aries (the self, new beginnings). The **four aces** piece (new beginnings)—are you sensing a theme here?—are splayed out. The **ace of diamonds** (spark, inspiration, news) lands on the bracelet, *trying to crawl in.* In fact, I only catch this later and note that, technically, the corner of the playing card places a ◆ in the seer's eye. **Citrine** (wealth, big money) touches the **ace of hearts** (desire, wish, happiness); **boot** (steps forward) touches the **ace of clubs** (goal, task, official document to be signed). **Ace of spades** (also means rebuilding after an ending) combines with the club. *C will receive money to begin a passionate new venture. This brings happiness. C, the day of this reading, received a call from the bank with great news. Her loan had been approved. She had the green light to begin building her new business. C will be busy. Exciting new developments will create some healthy space and flow between the two friends. C's being guided (cardinal) through an amazing new undertaking and career-oriented wish fulfillment.*

The cart's wheel of the **horse and cart** charm sits on C. The horse is working hard to drag both cart and C forward, toward the house of Pisces on the charmala (intense, phoenix energy, transformation). She's carting some heavy things there to be cleansed. C's also traveling away from the incident and (albeit it a bit reluctantly) entering the energy of the wisdom ring.

Finally, there's a small loop chain, and it's fallen with one twist. It touches the top of the bracelet. It has landed in the eighth house of Scorpio (transcendence). Holding a pointer over both letters *C* and *S* and extending their invisible lines, they intersect at this chain. C and S's paths will gladly cross again. It's close to the bracelet, so this will be soon. This isn't the end of their friendship—not at all. They'll have continued interaction; but in the short term, their connection has experienced a kink. C is in a difficult transition but has great things on her horizon including an opportunity to gain crucial traction on some old relationship patterns. The chain's formed a wonky lemniscate with two differently shaped loops. These two souls share many things in common, but they're very different people. Moving forward, they'll need a less judgmental assessment of their differences. Regardless, this happened for a reason.

The ◆ (fire) in an otherwise empty center carries the last whisper: There will be major changes in every area of C's life (four aces), including new people—even new love. It might not be easy, but it's the journey that matters in the end.

AFTERWORD

Well, here we all are, a few heartbeats away from the back cover. Just so you know, I've loved every second of hanging out with you. While I'd be honored to try and compose the finest words imaginable to say thank you and toodle pip, I think it only fitting to delegate this duty to the panoply of personalities that made this all possible: the trinkets, trifles, baubles, and bits.

Randomly selected, here they are: a mummy, a troll, a poppy, and an apple core, with what, from the bottom of their heart-shaped tin, they'd like to add:

Hello casters, old and new, we've got some parting words for you:

If at first, you feel a **dummy** . . .

Can't **see** squat? Your brain's all rummy?

Know that we're a waggish bunch, tricky, tacky, out-to-lunch.

Full of pranks and whoops-a-daisy. Happy when we make you crazy.

Truth be told, we know you're wise; We're *you*-obsessed. That's no surprise.

Here's to what the fates shall bring: Apples? Eggs? We've got this thing!

ABOUT THE AUTHOR

Tina Hardt is an author, diviner, and medium. She's the coauthor of *The Relative Tarot* with Carrie Paris, *The Sirens' Song: Divining the Depths with Lenormand & Kipper Cards* with Carrie Paris & Toni Savory, and *The Beloved Dead: An Oracle for Divining Ancestral Wisdom* with Carrie Paris.

Tina is a double Gemini who loves the great indoors, when she's not outdoors, inside her seer shed. Her prized collection of casting charms is easily in excess of 1,500 pieces and should be insured with Lloyd's of London. She lives in a purple house in Musselman's Lake in Whitchurch-Stouffville, Ontario, Canada, together with Roger, a beloved enabler, who finds the oddest things in the strangest places.

TO OUR READERS

Weiser Books, an imprint of Red Wheel/Weiser, publishes books across the entire spectrum of occult, esoteric, speculative, and New Age subjects. Our mission is to publish quality books that will make a difference in people's lives without advocating any one particular path or field of study. We value the integrity, originality, and depth of knowledge of our authors.

Our readers are our most important resource, and we appreciate your input, suggestions, and ideas about what you would like to see published.

Visit our website at *www.redwheelweiser.com*, where you can learn about our upcoming books and free downloads, and also find links to sign up for our newsletter and exclusive offers.

You can also contact us at *info@rwwbooks.com* or at

Red Wheel/Weiser, LLC
65 Parker Street, Suite 7
Newburyport, MA 01950